W9-CMU-246

WITHDRAWN

# Tell Me What to Eat if I Have Irritable Bowel Syndrome

# Tell Me What to Eat
# if I Have Irritable Bowel
# Syndrome

by

### Elaine Magee, M.P.H., R.D.

New York

**This edition published in 2009 by:**

The Rosen Publishing Group, Inc.
29 E. 21st Street
New York, NY 10010

Copyright © 2002 by Elaine Magee

First published as *Tell Me What to Eat if I Have Irritable Bowel Syndrome* by New Page Books / Career Press. End matter copyright © 2009 by The Rosen Publishing Group, Inc.

Cover design by Nelson Sá and Sam Zavieh

**Library of Congress Cataloging-in-Publication Data**

Magee, Elaine.
Tell me what to eat if I have irritable bowel syndrome / by Elaine Magee.
    p. cm.—(Tell me what to eat)
First published: Franklin Lakes, NJ : Career Press, 2000.
ISBN-13: 978-1-4042-1836-9 (library binding)
1. Irritable colon—Diet therapy—Juvenile literature. I. Title.
RC862.I77M24 2009
616.3'42—dc22

               2008014944

*Manufactured in the United States of America*

# Contents

**Introduction** ........................................................ 7

**Chapter 1:**
Everything You Ever Wanted to Ask
a Gastroenterologist ......................................... 12

**Chapter 2:**
Main Symptoms of Irritable Bowel Syndrome ................. 24

**Chapter 3:**
Everything You Ever Wanted to Ask
Your Dietitian About IBS .................................... 30

**Chapter 4:**
The 10 Food Steps to Freedom ........................... 47

**Chapter 5:**
The 20 Recipes You Cannot Live Without ....................... 70

**Chapter 6:**
Navigating the Supermarket ............................. 97

**Chapter 7:**
Restaurant Rules ......................................... 120

**Glossary** ............................................. 133

**For More Information** .................................. 135

**For Further Reading** .................................. 137

**Index** ................................................. 139

# Introduction

Being told you have irritable bowel syndrome (IBS) is a good news/bad news situation. The bad news is there is no real cure. The good news is that the condition will never kill you or seriously impair your health. In fact, approximately 60 percent of people with IBS symptoms never seek medical care. These people just live with it. I know, because I'm one of them. I'm a third-generation irritable bowel sufferer.

People with IBS have bowels that tend to overreact in certain situations. Whatever affects the bowels of the population at large, such as diet, hormones, or stress, affects those of IBS sufferers even more. And IBS symptoms are the result.

So what can we do? We can at least make ourselves feel more comfortable as we go through life with this syndrome. We can eat a healthful diet (rich in high-fiber foods that our systems tolerate), drink plenty of water, avoid foods that make us feel worse, and find ways to minimize and handle the stress in our daily lives.

But be forewarned, treating IBS is a little like trying to hit a moving target. Not only do IBS symptoms vary from one person to the next, they can also change from week to week in the same person. And when it comes to treatments, different things work for different people. The only way to know what works for you is to try it and see if it seems to help.

To make things even more complicated, the treatment you try for one symptom can cause a completely new symptom to occur. So with IBS, you definitely want to choose your treatments wisely. That's what this book is about: presenting the possible dietary treatments for IBS—many of which have helped IBS sufferers live more comfortable lives. People with IBS who don't seem to respond well to drugs or dietary modification may want to concentrate on the psychological treatments available for IBS. Individual or group psychotherapy, relaxation training, meditation, biofeedback, and hypnosis can all help relieve some symptoms.

## You are not alone

IBS has been around a while. Medical descriptions of IBS can be found from as far back as the late 1800s. If you have irritable bowel syndrome, you are not alone. In the United States alone, 25 to 55 million people suffer from some degree of IBS. Many of them don't even know that the symptoms they have been dealing with over the years have a name. After the common cold, IBS accounts for the most missed days of work, and up to 40 percent of all visits to gastro-enterologists are related to IBS symptoms. And what I find most interesting is that IBS is common across countries that are culturally very different from America, such as Japan, China, and India. So trust me, you are not alone.

# Bowels 101

Whether you are experiencing constipation or diarrhea, knowing how the colon is supposed to work will help you understand what's going on in your body. So let's review the jobs of the large and small intestines, which together are referred to as the bowel or bowels.

Once the stomach has churned food into mush, it releases small amounts of it into the small intestine. The bulk of the digesting and absorbing of the nutrients and calories from the food we eat happens in the small intestine. The pancreas contributes enzymes to help further digest food in general, and bile from the gallbladder and liver helps to break down fat in particular.

What's absorbed? Carbohydrates are broken down into sugars and absorbed. Protein is broken down into amino acids and absorbed. Fat is broken down into fatty acids and glycerol and absorbed. And vitamins and minerals, along with other important nutrients from the food we eat, are also absorbed into the bloodstream in the small intestine. What isn't absorbed? Fiber for one thing (more on this in other chapters).

The remaining food waste moves to the large intestine, which is also called the colon. The main job of the large intestine is to reabsorb water and salts as the food waste travels through it. This helps form solid stools, which can then theoretically exit the body a couple of days later via the rectum (easily and without discomfort).

These "movements" are controlled by nerves and hormones and by electrical activity in the colon muscle. Muscles in the colon help propel the food waste slowly toward the rectum. "Normal" bowel movements range from three stools a day to as few as three a week. A "normal" movement is one that is formed but not hard, contains no blood, and is passed without cramps or pain.

Sometimes there is too much water for the large intestine to reabsorb, or the food waste travels through the large intestine too quickly so the intestines don't have a chance to reabsorb enough water, resulting in frequent and/or watery stools (diarrhea). Sometimes there isn't enough water, or the food waste travels too slowly through the large intestine, resulting in infrequent and hard-to-pass stools (constipation).

## Identify sources of stress

Think back to when your IBS started. What was going on in your life? The majority of IBS patients report having a very stressful life event just before developing IBS. The event might be parents going through a divorce or separation, the death of a loved one, or changing jobs or locations.

Most people will tell you their irritable bowel symptoms are more pronounced when they are stressed. Therefore, if you have an irritable bowel, you must practice stress management and stress reduction as much as possible. Many of us don't even realize what is causing us stress. You might need some professional help to recognize your own personal stressors, such as jumping to conclusions, perfectionism, or seeing problems as catastrophes. Sometimes what we do in an effort to improve matters only makes the stress worse.

Obviously, this is a book about food and IBS, but there are nonfood suggestions that you can consider, too:

- Practice relaxation strategies (deep breathing, muscle relaxation, imagery, exercise, and so forth).
- Get the rest your body needs.
- Set your priorities realistically.
- Accept, adapt, and learn to let go.

- Work with your health care team (ideally a gastroenterologist, a psychologist, and a dietitian) to develop a treatment plan.

If you haven't already done so, please see your physician or a gastroenterologist to identify that you indeed have IBS, because there are many other gastrointestinal diseases that can have similar symptoms.

# Chapter 1

# Everything You Ever Wanted to Ask a Gastroenterologist

So you think you may have an irritable bowel. Depending on where you live, you may have to wait as long as a few months to see a gastroenterologist to confirm it. And when you do see one, chances are you'll forget to ask a few of your questions. Also, as time goes on, you might think up new questions. That's what this chapter is for.

**Q** **What is irritable bowel syndrome (IBS) and what are the symptoms?**

Twice as many women suffer from IBS than men. It usually develops in late adolescence or early adulthood. It affects up to 20 percent (one in five people) of the population in the Western world (*Lancet 340*[8833]: 1447-53, 1992). IBS is a common disorder of the intestines that can lead to:

- Crampy abdominal pain.
- Gassiness.

- Bloating.
- Changes in bowel habits (diarrhea, constipation, or both).
- A feeling of incomplete emptying of the bowel.
- Passing mucus with bowel movements.

Everybody's IBS is different. The symptoms can range from being mildly annoying (for most) to disabling (for a few).

The "irritable" bowel is more sensitive and reactive than a "regular" bowel. It begins to spasm after only mild stimulation or in situations that a normal bowel would not react to, such as:

- **Eating** (see tips on changing your eating style in Chapter 4). The simple act of eating causes contractions of the colon, normally causing an urge to have a bowel movement 30 to 60 minutes after a meal. With IBS, the urge can come sooner, along with cramps and diarrhea.
- **Distention from gas or other material in the colon** (for tips on avoiding gas-producing foods, see Chapters 3 and 4).
- **Certain medicines.**
- **Certain foods** (see tips in Chapters 3 and 4).
- **Stress**, which stimulates colonic spasms in people with IBS.

Some people have diarrhea (or several soft bowel movements) right after they wake up in the morning or right after they eat a meal. IBS symptoms may worsen in the presence of such stressors as travel, big social events, or changes in daily routine. For some, symptoms seem to get worse when they do not eat right or if they eat a big meal.

**Will my IBS eventually go away?**

Part of the nature of IBS is that it varies from person to person. Generally though, IBS symptoms fluctuate over time. In one study, more than half the IBS patients followed still had symptoms five years after they were first diagnosed with it. Some researchers report that almost one-third develop IBS after a bout of the stomach flu or food poisoning. In these cases, the symptoms are usually milder and can diminish over a three-to-five-year period.

**What causes IBS?**

IBS continues to mystify the experts. When colons of IBS sufferers are examined, there are no signs

---

**F.Y.I.** **Telltale Signs of Irritable Bowel Syndrome**

On a continual or recurring basis for at least 3 months:

• Abdominal pain or discomfort that is relieved with a bowel movement or that is associated with a change in frequency or consistency of stools.

• A varying pattern of defecation at least 25 percent of the time, with at least three of these characteristics:

  1. Altered stool frequency.
  2. A change in stool form (for example, from hard to loose and watery).
  3. Altered passage of stool (such as straining or urgency, or feeling incomplete evacuation).
  4. Passage of mucus.
  5. Bloating or sensation of having a distended abdomen.

of disease. Yet IBS can cause much pain and distress to the people who have it. Researchers are getting closer to the truth, though. They have discovered that the colon muscles of people with IBS begin to spasm after only mild stimulation. Their colons appear to be more sensitive, reacting strongly to events that would not bother most people, such as eating a large or rich meal or having a bit of gas in the colon.

Are you one of the women out there who seem to suffer from IBS-like symptoms only during menstruation? One-third of women who otherwise don't have gastro-intestinal (GI) symptoms have them only during their periods. Researchers suspect that reproductive hormones help trigger IBS symptoms, because about half of women with IBS report worsening symptoms—most often diarrhea—during their periods.

It is also possible that a lack of hormones could encourage IBS-like symptoms in some women. A recent study suggests that peri- and post-menopausal women have a high prevalence of IBS-like gastrointestinal complaints.

Experts also suspect that many people have a genetic predisposition to IBS. All I know is that I have a mild form of IBS, my mother has it, and her father had it. Sounds like a genetic link to me! New research also suggests that about one-third of IBS sufferers have a genetic mutation that is also linked to panic disorder.

Although scientists aren't certain why, childhood constipation and colic (as well as childhood physical or sexual abuse) increases the likelihood of developing IBS as an adult.

Possible causes of IBS:

- Autonomic motor dysfunction.
- Colonic motor dysfunction.
- Depressive disorder.
- Endocrine disease.

- Food allergy.
- Generalized neurological disorder.
- Small intestinal motor dysfunction.
- Psychological stress.
- Visceral sensory disorder.

**Is there a cure for IBS?**

So far there is no cure for IBS. But great strides have been made in managing the syndrome. Most people with IBS are able to control their symptoms by managing their stress, making dietary changes, and taking prescription medications as needed.

**Can medications relieve IBS symptoms?**

Let me start out by saying that there is no standard way of treating IBS and there is no drug in use anywhere that is a sure cure for the discomfort of an irritable bowel. However, there are some medicines that can help relieve symptoms in some people. Most doctors agree that medications are best used when symptoms are particularly troublesome or during special situations (such as when traveling).

Some doctors prescribe drugs that control colon muscle spasms, drugs that slow the movement of food through the intestines, or tranquilizers. Antidepressant drugs are sometimes used in patients who are also depressed.

For diarrhea, many physicians suggest beginning with loperamide (available over the counter as Immodium) and diphenoxylate plus atropine sulfate (Lomotil). Also, the cholesterol-lowering drug cholestyramine (Questran) brings sudden, dramatic relief for a few people who have persistent watery stools but no other IBS symptoms. These people have trouble properly absorbing bile acids (part of the digestive juices) and the drug acts by trapping and inactivating the bile acids so they cause less of a problem.

For people who don't have diarrhea or constipation but who have episodes of gut-wrenching pain, another drug may be helpful. Because bowel spasms are thought to account for this type of IBS pain, anticholinergic drugs such as atropine, propantheline (Pro-Banthine), or dicyclomine (Bentyl) may bring relief by blocking nerve signals that trigger bowel contractions. If the spasms always seem to occur after you eat a meal, taking the anticholinergic medication before the meal may stop them before they start.

Generally the use of laxatives (chemical stimulants) to help with constipation is discouraged because they can weaken the intestines and many people become dependent on them.

**Can medicines I take for other things be making my IBS worse?**

Sucralfate, calcium channel blockers, bismuth subsalicylate, and antacids containing aluminum can sometimes aggravate constipation. Other medicines can do the opposite and induce diarrhea. These include magnesium-containing antacids, lactulose, and sometimes psyllium and other fermentable fibers used as bulking agents (which can also worsen bloating).

**How do stress and anxiety affect IBS?**

Stress may worsen IBS symptoms, plain and simple. Stress stimulates colonic spasm in people with IBS. We don't completely understand why this happens but we do know that the colon is controlled in part by the nervous system and that the nervous system reacts to stress.

Stress-reduction (relaxation) training or counseling and support help relieve IBS symptoms in some people. But please understand you don't have IBS because you have a psychological problem. Remember, IBS is in large part a result of hypermotility and hypersensitivity of the colon.

One study showed that people with IBS scored higher in measures of anxiety and obsession, but not in measures of phobia, depression, somatic anxiety, and hysteria. The anxiety and obsession are thought to be the consequences, and not the causes, of the IBS symptoms.

 **Which types of psychotherapy might help?** Three types of treatments are yielding some success with IBS patients:

**1. Brief psychodynamic therapy** is conducted one on one with a psychiatrist or psychologist for a short time (such as once a week for two months). The goal of this therapy is to explore and identify potential unconscious factors that may be linked to IBS symptoms and to help the patient bring those factors into consciousness to better understand and control them.

**2. Cognitive behavioral therapy** is also performed by a psychiatrist or psychologist in either a group or one-on-one format. The purpose of this therapy is to teach people to cope a little less negatively with life's stressors. IBS sufferers are guided into identifying how they send themselves conscious negative messages. Maybe they take on more blame for situations than they should, or maybe they make things out to be worse than they really are. Patients are often asked to explore what areas of their lives are stressful and how they themselves contribute to the stress with their own perceptions. Repeated therapy sessions enable patients to gradually react more positively to the stressors in their lives—which translates into reduced bowel symptoms.

**3. Hypnosis** teaches people to use imagery to gain control over the muscles in their GI tracts. This can take place in a group or in one-on-one sessions under the direction of a psychiatrist or psychologist with hypnosis experience. Many patients using this method report less pain, bloating, cramping, diarrhea, and constipation.

If you would like to find a psychologist or psychiatrist with experience in treating IBS, the American Psychological Association can direct you to your state associations, which can refer you to a practitioner in your area. Call (800) 964-2000.

 **Does IBS lead to other intestinal diseases, such as cancer or colitis?**
No. Colitis refers to inflammation of the large intestine (colon). IBS does not involve nor cause inflammation of the colon. And IBS does not lead to cancer.

 **Could my symptoms indicate something else?**
If there is blood in your stool or if you have been having chills or fever, then you probably have something other than IBS.

A small number of people who think they have IBS could instead be suffering from a new family of disorders caused by hard-to-detect changes in the lining of the large intestine. With these disorders (microscopic colitis, collagenous colitis, and pericrypt eosinophilic enterocolitis), the colon looks normal. But if a bit of the tissue is examined under a microscope, inflammation or scarring can be seen.

Profuse watery diarrhea can be caused by something other than IBS. Frequently, and more often in women, it is actually due to laxative abuse. This is probably far more common than we know because people who abuse laxatives often keep it a secret from their physicians and families. Diarrhea can also be caused by rare, hormone-secreting tumors of the pancreas.

**Could I have a food allergy?**

Many of the clinical signs typical of intestinal food allergies and intolerance are the same as those that many people experience with irritable bowel syndrome. It is a good idea to find out if you have a food allergy or intolerance. A 1999 study in the *American Journal of Gastroenterology* found that more than 50 percent of the IBS patients studied were sensitized to some food or inhalant without showing any typical clinical signs. Usually the patients were unable to identify the potentially offending foods.

 **How long does it normally take for a meal to move through the digestive tract?**

Food passes through the esophagus and into the stomach almost immediately. However, it can take as long as three or four hours after a meal before the stomach completely empties into the small intestine. It can even take longer, depending on the size and fat content of the meal (larger and higher-fat meals stay in the stomach longer). The small intestine will take four to six hours to finish digesting a meal and absorbing its contents. It can take two to three days before food waste is finally formed into a stool and emptied from the rectum.

 **Why do I seem to have several bowel movements first thing in the morning?**

When you wake up in the morning, your bowel wakes up, too. Normal nerve connections trigger the large intestine to increase its activity (like after meals), particularly first thing in the morning.

**Q** **Can lack of sleep bring on symptoms in some IBS patients?**

(As answered by researcher W. Grant Thompson, MD, formerly with Ottawa Civic Hospital Division of Gastroenterology and co-author of *Fast Facts: Irritable Bowel Syndrome*. Santa Fe: Health Press, 2000.)

Lack of sleep is likely a result of some physical or mental stress and as such might trigger the experience of IBS symptoms, or make the individual less tolerant of them. Normally the gut is at rest during sleep, and it follows that daytime activities will continue at night if the patient remains awake. Moreover, we all know how much more troubling pain is when experienced at night.

---

**F.Y.I.** **When it probably isn't IBS**

These symptoms are not part of irritable bowel syndrome and probably indicate another problem and should be looked at immediately:

- Gastrointestinal bleeding.
- Fever.
- Weight loss.
- Nocturnal (occurring at night) symptoms.
- Fecal incontinence.
- Persistent severe pain.

**Q** **Can traveling bring on symptoms?**
(As answered by Dr. Thompson.)
The lack of physical activity while traveling long distances and the disruption of routine due to changing time zones and diet are bound to change gut rhythms. Constipation is a frequent result. Some extra dietary fiber and as much activity as a plane might permit will help prevent this. The effect is likely to be exaggerated in the person with IBS, where the gut tends to overreact to various stimuli.

At the other extreme is traveler's diarrhea, which is known to precede the onset of IBS. Some researchers believe that the nature of gut reactivity is altered by an attack of gastroenteritis. Although no histological changes are demonstrated in the IBS gut, there is reason to believe that certain inflammatory cells may continue to produce chemical mediators that alter gut behavior long after the original insult is gone.

**Q** **What medications can I use for traveling or times when my IBS is particularly severe?**
This is definitely something you want to work out with your gastroenterologist or internist, and it would depend on your symptoms. Some people experience constipation when they travel; others complain of diarrhea. One expert cited using 125 mg hyoscyamine sulfate, taken a half hour before meals and at bedtime, for rapid relief of hypermotility (food moving too fast through the intestines) and cramps.

**Do some IBS patients suffer from stomach-related symptoms during one of their intestinal "attacks"?**

(As answered by Dr. Thompson.)

The pain of IBS can be anywhere in the abdomen, even in the upper abdomen. Some patients also have accompanying nausea, bloating, and other gut symptoms. However, vomiting, weight loss, or anorexia should prompt a look for something other than IBS.

 Chapter 2

# Main Symptoms of Irritable Bowel Syndrome

**W**hat irritable bowel syndrome means to me could be, and probably is, quite different from what it means to you. Each of us experiences different symptoms with varying severity. Certainly though, specific symptoms do tend to be associated with irritable bowel syndrome. These symptoms are listed and discussed in this chapter.

## Abdominal pain

A typical pattern in IBS is the beginning of pain, soon followed by a somewhat formed bowel movement and relief (albeit temporary) of the pain. But shortly after this, the bowel spasms (causing pain), resulting in more watery bowel movements over several hours. The pain many people with IBS feel is often in the lower part of the abdomen, below the belly button, although some feel it throughout the abdomen. The pain often gets worse 60 to 90 minutes after meals. Research has shown that people with IBS have a lower pain threshold for gastrointestinal tract distension than people without IBS. However, their tolerance of other painful stimuli is at least equal to that of healthy controls. Therefore it is suggested that this pain may be due to a higher sensitivity of the bowel in people with IBS.

# Irregular pattern of defecation at least 25 percent of the time

This is a fancy way of saying there is a disturbance in the frequency, form (hard vs. loose/watery), or passage (straining, urgency, feeling of incomplete evacuation) of your stools some of the time. You are actually more likely to see episodes of irregular bowel function alternating with periods of normal bowel with an "irritable" bowel than you are with an "inflamed" or diseased bowel. You might have a regular bowel movement every day, except every fourth week or so your bowel movements are either more constipated or looser. Or you might only experience intestinal problems first thing in the morning or only late at night.

Some people suffer mainly from constipation; others primarily from loose stools. Still others suffer from both.

# Constipation-predominant IBS

Constipation-predominant IBS often starts in adolescence and may result from excessive colon contractions, which lead to stool dehydration (hard, stiff stools). People with this type of IBS seem to improve with a high-fiber eating plan. The goal is to consume around 30 grams of fiber a day, so many people have to use fiber supplements.

If you increase your fiber too fast, you might suffer from bloating and gas. To prevent this, you can use warm tap water enemas along with the fiber supplement. Also, your physician may add osmotic laxatives (glycerine suppositories, for example) or stool softeners if fiber alone isn't doing the trick. The use of stimulant laxatives is definitely discouraged.

There are some newer medications also being tested. Ask your physician about cisapride (the brand name is Propulsid) if you continue to have problems. Studies are showing it relieves abdominal pain and reduces abdominal distension.

## Diarrhea-predominant IBS

Maybe you wouldn't describe what you have as diarrhea; maybe the term "loose stools" is a little more accurate. Or maybe you have diarrhea sometimes and soft stools most of the time. Loose stools in IBS are usually of small volume but frequent. Having to go in the early morning or after meals, as well as stress-related urgency, is also common in people who experience this symptom.

I know that for me the early morning almost always offers a certain challenge. I usually have to go to the bathroom two or three times within the first hour after I wake up. This wouldn't be so bad if I didn't also have to make breakfast, pack two lunch boxes, get two girls ready for school, feed the dog, and let her out. I'm often in the middle of making toast when all of a sudden I have to hurdle over the doggy gate and make it around the corner to the closest bathroom.

This type of IBS may have something to do with what's going on inside the intestinal space (not the wall or muscle of the intestines). Carbohydrates, bile acids, short-chain fatty acids, or food allergens might be inside the intestines causing problems as they move through. Maybe they aren't being digested properly. Maybe they are being broken down by bacteria or causing water to move into the intestinal space. Soluble fiber may actually improve diarrhea for some by helping hold onto water when it is in the intestines (more on soluble fiber in Chapter 3 and 4).

## Mucus in the stool

Half of all IBS patients report mucus (without blood) in their stools. If you see blood mixed with mucus in the stool, this is not IBS; it is more likely to be colitis (inflammation of the colon). I know it is a bit alarming to find mucus in your stool, but mucus is normally produced by the intestine to serve as a lubricant. It's just that some people with IBS might be producing extra amounts.

## Abdominal bloating or swelling

Abdominal bloating or swelling is a common symptom in IBS, especially if you are constipated. The bloating usually worsens as the day goes on and improves after sleeping. If you are able to better manage your constipation or diarrhea, abdominal bloating and swelling may well subside.

## The feeling of incomplete emptying of the rectum

Most people who suffer from this symptom do in reality empty their rectums completely when they go to the bathroom. This symptom is a result of an oversensitive rectum, which causes a "false alarm."

## Gas attacks

For some people with IBS, it isn't the gas that bothers them as much as the abdominal pain and bloating that tend to come with it. Reducing the amount of gassy foods in your diet will help relieve abdominal pain, gas, and bloating.

Many gas-producing foods contain carbohydrates that are not completely digested in the small intestine. By the time they get to the end of the large intestine, bacteria (normally present in the intestines) have digested these carbohydrates and produced gas as a breakdown by-product.

However, some people with IBS may have a specific disturbance in bacterial fermentation and colonic gas production. Studies have found that gas production in the colon (hydrogen gas in particular) is indeed greater in people with IBS than the rest of the population.

## Symptoms occur or intensify during menstruation

For many women, IBS symptoms seem to be worse during their periods. Right before your period (if you can plan ahead) and certainly during it, it is especially important to avoid trigger foods or stressors that seem to bring on or aggravate bowel symptoms.

## Beyond the bowels: common IBS symptoms in other parts of the body

- Studies have shown that some people with IBS also have **heartburn**.

- Another symptom is **sleep disturbances**, which often aggravate IBS symptoms.
- **Fatigue** is a common complaint with IBS patients. Fatigue can be a result of disturbed sleep or exhausting periods of diarrhea, or it may indicate clinical depression or other serious psychological problems.
- **Bladder or urinary problems** are also associated with IBS. It may be that an irritable bowel causes a generalized sensitivity of the smooth muscle that lines the bowel and bladder.
- Non-cardiac **chest pain** (a sharp or dull ache in the central chest that cannot be ascribed to heart disease) sometimes also occurs in people with IBS.
- **Nausea**, **bloating**, or **pain in the upper abdomen** may be present.
- **Migraine headaches** have been linked to IBS. Smooth muscle, which lines the intestines, also lines the blood vessels that cause the throbbing effect of migraines. But beyond this, the mystery of why migraines and IBS are associated has not been solved.
- Some people with IBS also suffer from **fibro-myalgia**, a condition in which muscles and tendons have increased sensitivity and areas of tenderness and pain. With fibromyalgia, intense and persistent pain can be felt in the abdominal wall muscles.

# Chapter 3

# Everything You Ever Wanted to Ask Your Dietitian About IBS

A big part of treating and managing IBS involves what you eat, how and how much you eat, and where you eat. Certain foods and nutrients can help you and others can make your symptoms worse. This book is designed to help you discover which foods to emphasize and which not to touch with a 10-foot chopstick.

Remember while reading this chapter that IBS is a very individual disorder; you may have to try several treatments until you find one that works for you.

Even if your IBS is particularly affected by stress, you still need to know about the link between foods and IBS, because stressful times are when you need to pay the closest attention to your diet. Limiting your personal food triggers will help minimize the symptoms during the difficult time.

## Q Which changes in my diet might help relieve my symptoms?

There are foods to choose and foods to lose. People with mild, constipation-predominant IBS may benefit from an increase in soluble and insoluble fiber. Fiber can help because it improves the way the intestines work in some people. It may reduce bloating, pain, and other symptoms. Some people find more improvement with soluble-fiber foods. I happen to be one of them. I consider soluble fiber a gentler fiber; it forms a gel with water while in your intestines. You'll find a list of soluble-fiber food sources and supplements in Chapter 4.

To know which foods to lose, you will have to keep an FFS journal—of food, feelings, and symptoms—for a few weeks (more on this in Chapter 4). However, you may already have ideas about which foods aggravate your symptoms. You may find your symptoms worsen after you eat foods very high in fat or caffeine. Products containing sorbitol (an artificial sweetener used in sugar-free candy and gum) and antacids that contain magnesium can cause diarrhea. Beans, peas, cabbage, and some fruits give many people gas. Milk products can cause trouble in people with lactose intolerance or lactose maldigestion. Alcohol and high-sugar foods trigger symptoms for some.

## Q How do I know what my trigger foods are?

If you aren't sure which foods might be triggering your IBS symptoms, start by keeping an FFS journal for a couple of weeks. Play detective and try to find the links between the food, eating patterns, and symptoms. This is a very important step, which I'll discuss in greater detail in Chapter 4.

**Q** **What should you do if you suspect that a particular food is causing you problems?**
Totally avoid the suspected food for at least two weeks. Then try a small amount of it, either with foods you know you tolerate well or by itself. If you don't notice any symptoms, give it another day just to be sure. If you do notice symptoms, avoid it for another week and try it again (at a time when getting the symptoms wouldn't be terribly inconvenient) just to be sure.

**Q** **Why do some foods seem to bring on IBS?**
It is all too easy to say, "Avoid these foods," or, "These are bad foods for people with IBS and these are the good foods." The truth is, it just isn't that simple. Sometimes it isn't so much what you eat, but how much you eat, or how many trigger foods you eat in one meal or one day—or how much stress you're under while you eat. (Irritable bowel symptoms are more pronounced when you are stressed.) With IBS you may have to look beyond the specific foods to see the patterns, keeping in mind that the effects of trigger foods can often be unpredictable.
When looking for patterns, ask yourself:

- How much of the symptom-provoking food did you eat at one time?
- Did you eat two or more symptom-provoking foods at once?
- Did you eat one or more symptom-provoking foods at one meal and then one or more at the next meal?

**Q** **Do I need to cut any foods out of my diet if diarrhea is one of my main symptoms?**
You could try cutting out lactose-rich dairy products and sorbitol-containing diet products (like

sugar-free gum and mints) to see if the diarrhea improves. Other foods that tend to aggravate diarrhea are salads, bran products, beans, broccoli and related vegetables, apples, and excessive fat, alcohol, and caffeine.

### Q) Why do I develop symptoms after eating in restaurants or eating a big meal?

Having recently gotten a puppy, I am well aware that dogs need to relieve themselves, like clockwork, after a meal. The simple act of eating normally causes the muscles in the colon to contract. In people without IBS this might cause an urge to go to the bathroom 30 to 60 minutes after a meal. But in people with IBS, this feeling is more urgent and may come sooner— and with cramps and diarrhea. Does that mean you should eat as few meals a day as possible? Actually you should do the opposite—eat many smaller-sized meals.

You see, the greater the number of calories in the meal (especially from fat) the stronger the post-meal response tends to be. Food fat, from any source—animal or vegetable—is a strong stimulant of colon contractions. Generally, when we eat large, high-calorie meals, they also tend to be high in fat, delivering a double whammy to our intestines.

Eating out is particularly challenging for many people with IBS. Restaurant servings are usually large and the food is typically rich in fat and calories. For practical tips on eating out with IBS, check out Chapter 7.

### Q) Which foods or drinks, even in small amounts, bring on symptoms in some people with IBS?

Certain food substances, such as caffeine, alcohol, sorbitol, fructose, and fat, have gut effects even in healthy people. Their effects will be exaggerated in someone with IBS. If people without IBS have an uncomfortable reaction to a big bowl of baked beans, imagine what it could do to someone with IBS. Now, many experts hesitate to make lists of food triggers because they don't want to create a fear of certain foods. I don't either. But if you talk with people who have lived with IBS for years, they usually can name several foods or food substances that spell trouble for them. Those in the following list came up in several research and anecdotal sources, and have been known to give non-IBS sufferers trouble when eaten in large amounts.

- **Fructose** (the natural sugar found in fruits and berries) has been shown to increase abdominal distress in people with IBS. It is possible that the bacteria in the large intestine are breaking down the fructose that was not completely absorbed in the small intestine, resulting in gas, bloating, and/or diarrhea.

- **Soft drinks** containing large amounts of sugar (about 8 teaspoons per 12-ounce can) can wreak intestinal havoc in some people with IBS. Diarrhea is the main effect brought on by the high amount of sugar and possibly the caffeine. Cutting down to no more than one or two eight-ounce glasses per day might do the trick.

- **Sorbitol** (found naturally in some fruits and plants and used as a low-calorie sweetener because it isn't easily digested) can produce gas, bloating, diarrhea, and abdominal pain. You can find sorbitol in dietetic or sugarless products (dietetic jams and chocolate, sugarless gum, sugarless mints, and the like), as well as in peaches, apple juice, and pears.

- **Olestra** (a new, calorie-free fat substitute made from vegetable oils and sugar) is marketed under the brand name Olean and is used, so far, to make reduced-fat potato chips and crackers. Olestra is not digested or absorbed in the intestines and exits the body—and therein lies the problem. It can exit rather quickly in some people and bring on gas, bloating, diarrhea, and abdominal pain. You may be able to eat only small amounts of products containing Olestra.
- **Chocolate**, which does contain some caffeine and is obviously high in fat, has been linked to diarrhea and is listed in some references as something to be limited or avoided by people with IBS.

As for me personally, rarely is there a day when I don't have a little bite of chocolate. It is quite possibly the only food I actually crave. You can keep your chips, french fries, candy, and ice cream—all my body asks for is a bit of chocolate in the middle of the day. So believe me, it is with great pain that I list chocolate as a potential trigger food. I don't think it is a trigger for me personally, but then I only have a couple of bites a day (the equivalent of two chocolate Hershey's Kisses). Maybe if I had a whole chocolate bar, I would notice an effect.

One expert has noted that the main gut reaction to chocolate is heartburn, because it weakens the lower esophageal sphincter. Perhaps chocolate gives some people trouble because they tend to eat it in large quantities. A dietitian I spoke with remarked that some of her patients appear to be very sensitive to it. So I asked two of the dietitians I interviewed whether these people can tolerate small amounts of chocolate (such as 2 Hershey's Kisses), as opposed to an entire chocolate bar.

One said they probably could, and the other said that small amounts appear to be fine most of the time.

**Q** **Which fruits and vegetables tend to be well tolerated by the bowels?**
There are some general rules of thumb you can follow that can help make fruits and vegetables easier for your body to handle. *Vegetables should be cooked* to reduce potential gas production and *fruits should be canned* (in juice or light syrup) or *eaten ripe*, when the fruit and skin are soft. For specific suggestions, refer to the following list.

# Vegetables to try (cooked):

| | | |
|---|---|---|
| asparagus* | mushrooms | pumpkin* |
| beets | potatoes* | zucchini |
| carrots* | sweet potatoes* | |
| green or yellow beans | spinach* | |
| green peas | winter squash* | |

---

\* high in vitamin A (carotene), vitamin C, and/or folate
(folic acid)

---

**F.Y.I.** **Vegetables and Vitamin C**

Tomatoes and tomato juice, which are high in vitamin C, are tolerated by people who don't suffer from acid reflux or heartburn.

Baked potatoes (also high in vitamin C) are usually well tolerated, with or without the skin, even when a moderate amount of margarine, butter, or grated cheese is added.

# Fruits to try:

| | |
|---|---|
| canned fruit | nectarines |
| peeled apples | kiwi |
| applesauce | orange/orange juice* |
| soft, ripe bananas | peaches |
| grapefruit/grapefruit juice* | pears |

\* high in vitamin A (carotene), vitamin C, and/or folate (folic acid)

**Q** **Which foods are particularly helpful when you are having an IBS episode?**

The BRAT diet, prescribed by pediatricians for children recovering from diarrhea, can help. BRAT stands for Bananas, Rice, Applesauce, and Toast. Most people with diarrhea also benefit from other bland foods, such as boiled or poached eggs, crackers, and gelatin.

Getting enough water or other fluids is crucial in order to prevent dehydration from diarrhea. Signs of dehydration include a decrease in the need to urinate, dark or light brown urine, sunken eyeballs, rapid pulse, vomiting, constant thirst, drowsiness, and even unconsciousness.

**Q** **If I lower the fat in my favorite foods, will I be able to tolerate them better?**

Many people I spoke with said yes. Fat in food is known to exaggerate the gastrocolonic response, so greasy

---

 **Caution . . .**

If you have acid reflux or heartburn, citrus fruits may cause some discomfort.

or high-fat foods can be problematic for some people with IBS. But that doesn't mean you have to banish your favorite foods forever. Reduced-fat pizza and ice cream, and light (but delicious) recipes for foods like lasagna and fried chicken, might fit into your food plan very nicely.

**Q** **What is it about my eating style that might be aggravating my IBS?**
Some symptoms of IBS can be linked to *how* you eat more than *what* you eat. Consider the following questions and then ask yourself whether you can modify your behavior.

- **Do you eat too quickly?** If you do, you might be eating a lot at one time because it is harder to be aware of how much you are eating, how your body feels, and whether you are satisfied.

- **Do you go to fast-food chains often?** If you like going to fast-food restaurants, you might just need to change what you order. Fast food is typically high fat, which can cause indigestion, abdominal pain, and even diarrhea in some people. Choosing items that are lower in fat often helps most people. But it is possible that something other than the amount of fat (such as preservatives) is aggravating your symptoms.

- **Do you skip meals or eat a lot of food one day and very little the next?** This type of eating style can encourage irritable bowel symptoms such as bloating, abdominal pain, and irregular bowel movements. It is also particularly likely to cause gas.

- **Are you a junk-food junkie?** Junk food (chips, cheese puffs, and candy bars) is high in fat and calories but offers very little in the way of nutrition. These popular snacks can be hard to digest, leading to indigestion, gas, diarrhea, and abdominal pain.

- **Do you sometimes overeat?** People with irritable bowels often become highly symptomatic after eating large amounts. You may have noticed that during or after holidays, when many of us eat much more than our stomachs can possibly hold, you end up with indigestion, bloating, abdominal pain, and/or nausea. This could very well be because you tend to overeat at holiday meals (which also tend to be high in fat).

## Q | Is there anything I can add to my diet to discourage IBS symptoms?

Not getting enough fiber or water on a daily basis can aggravate some IBS symptoms. There is evidence that at least 30 grams of fiber a day will improve constipation and some other symptoms.

People with IBS are a lot more likely to meet this fiber goal in the future, because we have extra motivation to do it. If getting enough fiber helps alleviate some of our IBS symptoms, you better believe we are going to make sure we get enough fiber. I notice the difference when I don't get enough fiber.

High-fiber diets can keep the colon slightly distended—which is actually a good thing, because it is thought to help prevent spasms. Soluble fiber, which dissolves in water and keeps water in the stools, helps prevent hard, difficult-to-pass stools. I personally think of soluble fiber as the gentler fiber. While in your intestines it holds on to water and forms a gel (slowing down the passage of food—usually a good thing with IBS suffers) then moving toward the end of the intestines in an orderly fashion.

But what about bran? Bran is an insoluble fiber that does not dissolve in water. Some trials report an improvement in constipation with bran. In sufficient amounts, bran is supposed to soften stools and prevent straining during elimination. However, one study found that 55 percent of patients reported that bran made their IBS worse. Besides wheat bran, you can get insoluble fiber by eating unpeeled fruits, whole grains, and most vegetables.

Don't forget to drink plenty of water and increase your fiber slowly to avoid the gas and bloating that can accompany a quick increase in fiber. (Even if this does happen, it will dissipate after a few weeks as your body adjusts to the change.)

 **Which foods can I eat that are high in gentler, soluble fiber?**
The following foods contain soluble fiber:
- Psyllium seed and psyllium products.
- Beans.
- Oats.
- Barley.
- Apples.
- Bananas.
- Citrus fruits.
- Carrots.
- Green beans.

 **Are there any herbs that might help my symptoms?**
There are some natural anti-spasmodics out there. Fresh mint leaves, for example, when brewed into a strong tea, can help some people.

**How is lactose intolerance related to IBS?**
The common symptoms of lactose intolerance are nausea, cramps, bloating, gas, and diarrhea. So you can see how easy it would be to confuse lactose intolerance for IBS and vice versa. The lactose intolerance symptoms will arise anywhere from 30 minutes to two hours after eating or drinking something containing lactose, the sugar in milk.

Lactose is normally broken down into smaller sugars, which are then absorbed in the small intestine. People who are lactose intolerant do not digest lactose well because they do not produce enough lactase, the enzyme that breaks down the lactose. Without enough lactase, some of the lactose isn't being broken down and absorbed. This leftover lactose ends up in the large intestine, where it has no choice but to interact with bacteria, resulting in the production of short-chain fatty acids and—what else—gas (mostly hydrogen and carbon dioxide).

If gas wasn't enough, lactose-intolerant people also end up with diarrhea, because lactose, which shouldn't be in the large intestine, attracts water. Extra water in the intestines makes for watery stools. The combination of gas and watery stools is often described as "explosive diarrhea" (that conjures up some undesirable images, doesn't it?).

Between the ages of 5 and 14, many people in America and other parts of the world seem to experience a genetically programmed reduction in lactase synthesis to about 10 percent of the activity they had in infancy. About 25 percent to 30 percent of the U.S. adult population has low lactase activity and could be described as having lactose maldigestion. Certain ethnic groups are more likely to develop it though, with as many as 75 percent of African-Americans and Native Americans and 90 percent of

Asian-Americans being lactase-deficient. It is least common among people of northern European descent.

Just like with IBS, the degree of lactose intolerance varies from person to person. Millions of people suffer from lactose intolerance and don't realize it. And many people think they are lactose-intolerant and are really not. Mildly lactose-intolerant people, for example, may only experience a little extra gas or slight diarrhea when they eat or drink a little too much lactose.

For people with lactose intolerance, there is a rule of thumb to keep in mind: The more lactose you consume, the more severe the symptoms (depending on your particular lactose threshold/tolerance level). Many people with lactose intolerance can handle a small amount of lactose. They can often consume the equivalent of up to two cups of milk a day, as long as the milk is taken in two doses, spaced many hours apart, and consumed with other foods.

If you think you might have a problem digesting lactose:

1.  **Find out for sure whether you are lactose intolerant.** You can do this with one of two fairly simple tests at your doctor's office. In the hydrogen breath test, patients drink a high-lactose liquid and their breath is analyzed at regular intervals. It works because undigested lactose in the colon is fermented by bacteria, producing hydrogen. The hydrogen travels through the bloodstream to the lungs and is exhaled. Another test is the stool acidity test, which measures the amount of acid in a stool sample. It works because undigested lactose fermented by bacteria in the colon creates lactic acid and other short-chain fatty acids, which can be measured in the stool.

2. **Find out how much lactose you can comfortably consume.** How much dairy can you handle at one time, and how many times a day can your body manage it without symptoms? Unfortunately the only way to answer this is through trial and error.

- Start with small amounts of dairy and work your way up.
- Pay attention to the amount of lactose, rather than the amount of dairy products you are eating or drinking, because some dairy products have much less lactose than others.
- Don't consume dairy products by themselves. Have them with other foods.

3. **Experiment with lactase tablets to see if they help you.** There are several products available; look for them in your local pharmacy. Just one little LACTAID Ultra Caplet, for example, works quickly to help you easily and comfortably digest the lactose your body can't quite handle. Just take a caplet with your first bite of dairy foods. You can use it every day, with every meal, if you like.

---

**F.Y.I.    But I used to be able to drink milk**

Are you wondering if you weren't lactose intolerant before, why are you now? Certain illnesses can create a lactase deficiency later in your life. This sudden deficiency, coupled with an already declining level of lactase (as we age), can give us a type of lactose intolerance. What type of illness? Scientists suggest that certain infections can change the ecology of the GI tract.

**How much lactose is in there?**
Many people can manage low-lactose dairy foods, such as ice cream and aged cheeses, but not other dairy products. Some people are perfectly fine with a serving of yogurt, even though it contains about 12 grams of lactose, because the bacterial cultures used in making yogurt produce lactase.

Here's a rule of thumb on dairy and lactose that will leave some people jumping for joy: The higher the fat content of a dairy product, the lower the lactose level tends to be. Rich ice cream tends to be better tolerated than light ice cream or ice milk, and whole milk is usually better tolerated than low-fat and skim milk. By the way, some IBS sufferers say they tolerate chocolate milk (the only kind of milk you'll ever see me drinking) better than plain milk. (The mechanism by which cocoa helps lactose digestion is not yet known.)

|                      | Serving Size | Lactose (g) |
| -------------------- | ------------ | ----------- |
| Milk (whole)         | 8 ounces     | 11.4g       |
| Milk (1% or 2%)      | 8 ounces     | 11.7g       |
| Milk (skim)          | 8 ounces     | 11.9        |
| Yogurt (plain)       | 8 ounces     | 12 g        |
| Ice cream/ice milk   | 8 ounces     | 5-7 g       |
| Sour cream           | 4 ounces     | 4 g         |
| Processed cheese     | 1 ounce      | 2 g         |
| Hard cheese          | 1 ounce      | 1 g         |
| Butter               | 1 teaspoon   | trace       |

# Hidden lactose

People with a very low tolerance for lactose sometimes need to avoid food products that contain small amounts of lactose, such as:

- Bread and bread products.
- Cakes, brownies, and cookies.
- Processed breakfast cereals.
- Instant potatoes, soups, and breakfast drinks.
- Margarine.
- Lunch meats (except for kosher ones).
- Salad dressings.
- Candies and snack foods.
- Mixes for pancakes, biscuits, and cookies.

Avoid products containing whey, curds, milk by-products, dry milk solids, and non-fat dry milk powder, as well as, of course, milk. Be aware that 20 percent of prescription drugs and about 6 percent of over-the-counter medicines contain some lactose.

**Q** **Because I have IBS I am particularly fearful of getting colon cancer. How can I modify my diet to help prevent this?**
Saturated and animal fats, red meat, and protein are implicated as contributing factors in developing colon cancer. Total caloric intake may also play a part. And high consumption of animal fat, particularly of red meat, has been correlated with increased risk.

Some studies have shown that insoluble fiber helps protect against colon cancer. Fiber increases stool bulk, which decreases transit time and dilutes the stool, thereby reducing contact time between the potential carcinogens and the intestinal wall. Fiber also binds with bile acids and carcinogens, possibly reducing the likelihood that they will do any damage.

However, more than any other dietary component, vegetables have been shown most consistently to protect against colon cancer. A protective effect from vegetables was demonstrated in 80 percent of 28 studies. Fruits and vegetables contain an abundant array of recognized nutrients and phytochemicals (plant compounds that may decrease the risk of cancer). Evidence suggests that many of the phytochemicals in plants have anti-cancer effects in the human body.

 Chapter 4

# The 10 Food Steps to Freedom

We know that irritable bowel symptoms range from constipation to diarrhea and that symptom severity varies from person to person. We know that different food strategies help different people. We also know many studies have failed to show that particular foods cause IBS. But does that mean there isn't anything we can do to help manage our symptoms? Of course not.

There are foods that do affect intestinal activity, even in people with normal bowels. It makes sense that these effects will be exaggerated in someone with IBS, whose intestines may react more strongly to various stimuli.

The basic strategy to the 10 food steps to freedom is to minimize these food effects and keep our bowels healthy. We can work to slow down the very fast bowel and to gently speed up the very slow bowel. Try the steps for at least six weeks, as it can take that long for your body to adjust and respond. These food steps might be enough to help manage milder conditions, in which the symptoms are occasional, stress related, or caused by too much food or drink.

Because everyone's irritable bowel syndrome is unique to him or her, consider these three keys to managing your symptoms:

1. Understand the links between diet, stress, and your symptoms.
2. Match possible management strategies to your symptoms.
3. Pay close attention to which strategies seem to help which symptoms.

The first food step to freedom involves keys 1 and 3. The rest of the food steps will arm you with diet strategies that can help you manage your symptoms, key 2. Some food steps may be more helpful to you than others. Choose whichever work for you.

# Food Step 1: Keep an FFS Diary (Food, Feelings, and Symptoms)

Keep a log of what you eat and drink, your feelings, and your irritable bowel symptoms for a couple of weeks. The information will help you (and perhaps your medical team) identify foods and eating patterns that trigger your symptoms.

## About feelings and stress

- General feelings and worries can influence how you experience your irritable bowel symptoms.
- Stress may not affect the bowel until several days after you experience it.

- Stress may not affect the bowel to the same degree, and in the same way, each time.
- In this modern, busy life most of us lead, we have become so used to stress so we have trouble identifying it. Ask yourself what was stressful about your day and if there are any events or feelings you want to note.

## Writing the diary entry

Choose a set time each day to write in your FFS diary. You might prefer the end of the day, when things tend to be calm and you have a bit of time to yourself. You can think back over the day and write down what you ate and drank, how you felt, whether you were stressed, and any IBS symptoms you experienced, including time of day and severity. (You can find a blank entry form on page 50.)

# Food Step 2:
# Eat high-fiber foods (as tolerated)

Notice that this food step doesn't say, "Eat fiber" it says "Eat high-fiber foods." We know that both types of fiber benefit our bodies in many ways. But there are other nutrients and phytochemicals in high-fiber foods that help fight cancer

---

### F.Y.I.  How much fiber?

The National Cancer Institute and the U.S. Food and Drug Administration recommend between 25 and 30 grams of fiber per day.

# FFS Diary

Day_____

| Time | Foods/Drink (write amounts) | Symptoms/Severity | Stress/Feelings |
|------|------|------|------|
|  |  |  |  |
|  |  |  |  |
|  |  |  |  |
|  |  |  |  |
|  |  |  |  |
|  |  |  |  |
|  |  |  |  |
|  |  |  |  |
|  |  |  |  |
|  |  |  |  |
|  |  |  |  |
|  |  |  |  |
|  |  |  |  |
|  |  |  |  |
|  |  |  |  |
|  |  |  |  |
|  |  |  |  |

## Notes
Possible food triggers

_____

_____

_____

_____

_____

and heart disease as well. You'll read more about some of these later in the chapter.

In order for a high-fiber eating plan to work its magic, you have to *follow it (almost) every day*. Also, it will work better if you *spread your high-fiber foods throughout the day*.

Don't try to make up for all the fiber you've been missing in a matter of hours. *Start with small quantities* of high-fiber foods and slowly increase up to 25 to 30 grams a day.

One more thing: You shouldn't increase your fiber without increasing fiber's partner—water. *Drink plenty of liquids* (preferably those without caffeine, alcohol, or a lot of sugar). See food step 3 for details.

# Fiber's role in the intestines

Fiber is made up of complex carbohydrates that are not digestible by human enzymes. It is one of the last components of a meal to leave the stomach. The body holds on to the fiber in the stomach as long as it can so that the fiber doesn't interfere with the digestion/absorption of the other food components that are going on further down in the intestines.

When the fiber makes it down to the large intestine, bacterial enzymes normally present in the intestines try to break some of it down. Nutrients from this breakdown are absolutely crucial for the normal health of the cells that line the large intestine. (Gas can also be a by-product of this bacterial breakdown of fiber.)

# If you suffer from periodic constipation or diarrhea

It doesn't come as a surprise that people with irritable bowel syndrome who battle periodic constipation benefit from high-fiber diets. When we think of constipation we think of needing roughage. But actually, if you suffer from the diarrhea type of IBS, a gentle fiber supplement and bulking agent, such as psyllium, may be helpful, too. It can add many grams of fiber quickly and painlessly.

There are several psyllium products on the market, but you should be aware that they can produce bloating in some people. I have been using Perdiem, a psyllium supplement, before bed and have found it helps minimize my morning symptoms without any bloating or other side effects. For those who do have problems with psyllium, there are synthetic bulking agents (poly carbophil or methyl cellulose) that are supposed to be less likely to produce bloating.

Start with half the suggested dosage and increase over the next few days until you reach the full dose. For example, the Perdiem instructions suggest that adults and children 12 years and older take one to two rounded teaspoons once or twice a day. Work up to this dosage by starting with a rounded half teaspoon once or twice a day. After a couple of days, increase to one teaspoon once or twice a day, and after a couple more days, increase to

---

### F.Y.I. Never heard of Psyllium?

Psyllium is a grain grown in India. Its seeds happen to be high in soluble fiber. Since the early 1900s, American pharmaceutical companies have been making over-the-counter bulk-formers from psyllium seed.

**WARNING:** Some people have an allergic reaction to psyllium, ranging from stuffy noses, itchy eyes, coughing, and wheezing to (very rarely) anaphylactic shock. So start with very small amounts until you know you are not allergic.

1.5 teaspoons once or twice a day. Finally, a few days later, increase to two teaspoons once or twice a day.

# 7 fiber tips for people with irritable bowels:

1. Try to eat about three servings of whole grains or whole-grain products (breads, rolls, crackers, muffins, or cereal) each day. Over recent years, scientists have credited most of whole grains' health attributes to their fiber. We also now know the nutrients and phytochemicals found in whole grains play a role in preventing cancer and heart disease. Whole grains contain:

   - **Lignans**—which appear to function as antioxidants, preventing cellular changes that can lead to cancer.
   - **Flavonoids**—which may reduce the risk of heart disease.
   - **Tocotrienols**—which are powerful antioxidants that help prevent the formation of dangerous cholesterol.
   - **Saponins**—which may bind with cholesterol in the digestive tract and escort it out of the body.
   - **Vitamin E**—which is an important antioxidant and has been linked to reducing the risk of heart disease and some cancers.
   - **Minerals** (zinc, selenium, copper, iron, manganese, and magnesium)—which help protect body cells against damage from oxygen.

2. Find out which type of fiber works best for you— soluble or insoluble. (Oatmeal and barley are rich in soluble fiber; other whole grains are rich in

insoluble fiber). Both fibers benefit our bodies, but in different ways (see box on page 55), so getting a combination is generally best for the public at large. But what about people with IBS? Although some experts recommend focusing on insoluble fiber for irritable bowels, the soluble fiber grains (oats, barley, psyllium) are still well tolerated and fine for most people with IBS. In fact, some people fare better with soluble fiber than insoluble.

3. Choose one concentrated source of fiber each day:

   • **A high-fiber cereal**, such as All Bran, 100% Bran, or Bran Buds with Psyllium. Start with a quarter cup per day for seven to 10 days, then increase to half a cup per day. You may want to mix the high-fiber cereal with a lower-fiber cereal you like.

   • **Natural bran.** Start with two tablespoons per day for seven to 10 days, then increase to four tablespoons a day. Add to cereals, smoothies, baked goods, whatever you can.

   • **Bulking agent or fiber supplement** (without a stimulant) such as Metamucil, Perdiem, Normacol, or Citrucel. Start with one rounded (not heaping, not level) teaspoon each day for seven days, then increase by adding another teaspoon at another time of day for seven days. You may need to add another teaspoonful at a different time of day so that you get to about one teaspoon three times a day.

4. Don't have most of your fiber all at once—spread your fiber foods/supplements throughout the day.

5. Focus on getting fruits and vegetables (that have fiber and important nutrients) that are better tolerated and tend not to form gas in people with IBS (for a list, see Chapters 2 and 3).

6. Drink eight or more eight-ounce glasses of water every day (see food step 2 for details).

7. Give it time. It takes the intestinal tract up to six weeks to adapt to a new, higher-fiber food plan. However, your intestines might never adjust to some foods, such as cabbage or certain beans.

# Fitting in fiber

- Toss a handful of fruit on pancakes, waffles, french toast, yogurt, ice cream, and cereal.

---

### F.Y.I.  What does each type of fiber do for you?

Fiber does a whole lot more for our bodies than just keeping things moving.

**Soluble fiber:** Oats, beans, psyllium, and some fruits and vegetables (carrots, apples, citrus).
Lowers cholesterol; helps reduce risk of diabetes.

**Insoluble fiber:** Husks of whole grains, wheat bran, and stalks and peels of fruits and vegetables.
May help reduce risk of colorectal cancer, diverticular disease, varicose veins, hemorrhoids, and obesity.

**Fiber** also helps us eat less by lowering insulin, an appetite stimulant, and by making us feel full.

- Add beans to soups, casseroles, salads, and anything else you can think of.

- Use fresh spinach leaves to make your green salads. It has two to three times more fiber than iceberg lettuce.

- Read the label on your bread to see how much fiber it really contains. Some breads sound like they have a lot of fiber but they really don't.

- There are a few brands of frozen waffles with an impressive fiber total. Look for the whole-wheat or whole-grain types and check the grams of fiber on the label.

- Get dipping. Either dip raw vegetables in salad dressing or ranch dip (reduced fat or made with canola oil is best) or make your dip your fiber source—dip crackers or chips into a bean dip.

- Add fruits everywhere you can. Even dried fruit will work to boost fiber.

- Add vegetables every chance you get—even on your pizza!

# Food Step 3: Drink eight or more 8-oz. glasses of water

Caffeine-free liquids, such as juice, milk, herbal tea, and non-caffeinated soft drinks, can count toward two of the eight glasses of water per day. The rest has got to be good, old-fashioned $H_2O$. Healthy bowels need plenty of water to be able to do their job right. And if you are following food step 2 and eating plenty of fiber, drinking more water is even more essential—the two go hand in hand.

I know it is difficult to drink all those glasses of water. I myself have to work on it every day. These tricks have helped me:

- I keep bottles of water in my car.
- I try to drink a glass of water right when I wake up (it's one of the first things I do) and another one right before I go to bed. That's two glasses right there.
- I like to drink "fun water" every day, too. I treat myself to a glass of seltzer water with ice and a slice of lemon, or a glass of flavored (unsweetened) mineral waters (it comes in such flavors as lime, lemon, and cola berry).
- Find a decaffeinated tea that you really like. Then make a batch of iced tea to keep in the refrigerator. I enjoy peach-ginger hot tea; for iced tea, I like to use Good Earth's regular decaf tea bags.

# Food Step 4: Limit caffeine

Coffee is an example of a drink that you may tolerate only in small amounts or not at all. Why? Coffee contains caffeine, and caffeine stimulates the muscles in the digestive tract. That morning cup of joe gives your intestines a jolt along with your brain. You may have noticed how it seems to wake up your large intestine about 30 to 60 minutes after you drink it. Caffeine also stimulates the kidneys, causing them to release more water into the bladder than needed. This diuretic effect certainly seems to counteract everything in food step 3, doesn't it?

The number-one source of caffeine in the American diet is coffee. Second in line are colas and other soft drinks. How do you get around this? Drink primarily decaffeinated coffee to minimize muscle stimulation and dehydration from coffee. Be aware, though, that you still may suffer stomach pain or heartburn from it.

I like my coffee just as much as the next gal, but as far back as I can remember, I've been drinking decaf. I noticed way back when that when I drank coffee I had trouble sleeping and would get jittery, weak, and light-headed within an hour. Not exactly the effect I was looking for. I personally don't depend on coffee for a pick-me-up. I just happen to love its flavor, so decaf easily satisfies me.

# How much caffeine is in there?

| Beverage | Caffeine (mg) |
| --- | --- |
| Coffee, 6 ounces | |
| Automatic percolated | 70-140 |
| Filter drip | 110-180 |
| Instant, regular | 60-90 |
| Instant, decaffeinated | 0-6 |
| Tea, 6 ounces | |
| Made weak | 20-25 |
| Made strong | 80-110 |
| Cola (12-ounce can) | 20-60 |

# Food Step 5:
## Avoid high-fat meals and snacks

I'm afraid IBS is yet another reason not to eat lots of fatty foods. Fat in food is known to exaggerate the gastrocolonic response. Fat is harder to digest, so the higher the fat content of your meal, the longer it tends to stay in the stomach before moving on to the intestines.

You may have already noticed that large amounts of fat eaten in one meal can cause your bowel to be somewhat irritable. Does that mean you need to go fat free all the way and treat fat as the enemy? Absolutely not. You can have your fat and eat it, too—just don't go overboard.

Remember that fat is better tolerated when eaten in small amounts throughout the day rather than all at once. You are going to have to work out what this means to you personally in terms of your food choices and your symptoms.

I have personally noticed that I can be quite comfortable eating half an order of tempura (Japanese battered and fried shrimp and vegetables). But if I eat the entire order, I'm done for. And if I go to a restaurant, I can do well if I order just one dish that is high in fat. But if I also eat a rich dessert and perhaps a high-fat appetizer or side dish, troubles are sure to follow.

What about making high-fat favorite foods lower in fat? Does that make them easier on the bowels? Clinicians tell me that for many people the answer is yes. My own experience has shown me that this is true for me. So, for example, a lower-fat spaghetti made with very lean ground beef and mild seasonings will probably go down better than a spaghetti made with greasy, spicy sausage. Or you might find that you feel fine after eating an extra-lean burger made at home with oven-baked steak fries, but that you definitely do not after eating a bacon cheeseburger and fries at a diner. Keep this in mind when you look over your FFS diary.

You will find ideas to help you avoid high-fat meals in Chapter 6 (supermarket tips) and Chapter 7 (tips for eating out). For ideas when cooking at home, take a look at the following information and the recipes in Chapter 5.

# How low can you go?

How much fat can you cut and still maintain the taste and texture of the original recipe? Each recipe has an *ideal fat threshold*, the minimum amount of oil, butter, margarine, or shortening needed to produce a food that tastes like its fat-laden original. If you go below this ideal amount of fat or if you don't use a suitable fat replacement, you won't be happy with the results. I've been "lightening" recipes for 15 years and I've written six cookbooks, so trust me on this.

Over the years, I have developed ideal fat thresholds and fat replacements for different types of recipes. Take a look below.

# My favorite fat replacements

*Ideal fat replacements* are the fat-free or lower-fat ingredients best used to replace fat removed from a recipe. The following ingredients constitute my fat replacement arsenal. You will recognize some of these from the table on pages 62 to 63. All of these foods add flavor and moisture with little or no fat. I believe there is an ideal fat replacement for each recipe. For example, I might use lemon yogurt as a fat replacement in corn bread and maple syrup as a fat replacement when making chicken sausages. I tend to use light sour cream as a fat replacement in brownies, but I prefer to use fat-free cream cheese as a fat replacement in cookies. I might use coffee liqueur as a fat replacement in a graham cracker pie crust.

### Buttermilk

Buttermilk makes a nice fat replacement in certain recipes because it is thick and adds a distinctive, pleasantly sour flavor. I always buy the smallest container, because it tends to spoil rather quickly.

### Chocolate syrup

While it may sound high in fat, chocolate syrup is virtually fat free and contains about 40 to 50 calories per tablespoon. Use it instead of some of the oil or melted butter in cakes or brownies. You can reduce the granulated sugar called for in the recipe to compensate for the added sweetness from the chocolate syrup.

## Cream cheese (fat free or light)

Fat-free cream cheese makes a nice replacement for butter or shortening when the thick richness of fat is crucial, as is the case with cookies, rich cakes, frostings, pie crusts, or biscuits.

## Flavored low-fat yogurt

I like to use flavored low-fat yogurt as a fat replacement for oil in quick breads and sometimes in cakes and coffee cakes. You can have a lot of fun with the different flavors; try coffee or vanilla in a chocolate cake and lemon or orange in a spice cake.

## Light or fat-free sour cream

I use light or fat-free sour cream as a fat replacement for butter or shortening in cakes and brownies (and sometimes dressings, gravies, and such).

## Lemon juice

I like to use lemon juice in place of most of the oil in marinades or salad dressings, and even in cakes or quick breads, because it adds a lot of flavor, even in small amounts.

## Fruits and fruit purees

I use crushed fruit, such as crushed pineapple, or fruit purees, such as applesauce or apple butter, when their flavors complement the other ingredients in a particular recipe. For example, I'll use crushed pineapple in place of some of the oil in a carrot cake, or apple butter instead of half the butter in a spice or coffee cake.

# Ideal fat thresholds and fat replacements for different types of recipes

| Recipe | Fat Threshold | Fat Replacements |
|---|---|---|
| Biscuits | 4 tablespoons shortening for every 2 cups flour. | Fat-free cream cheese, non-fat or light sour cream. |
| Cake mixes | No additional fat is needed because most mixes already have 4 grams of fat per serving; replace the oil that is called for with one of the fat replacements listed. | Non-fat or light sour cream, applesauce, pineapple juice, or liqueur, depending on the cake. |
| Homemade cakes and coffee cake | 1/4 to 1/3 cup shortening or butter per cake. | Liqueur for some cakes, light sour cream for chocolate ones; fruit juice or purees work well with carrot, apple, and spice cakes. |
| Cheese sauce | Omit butter; the cheese is the vital fatty ingredient; use a sharp, reduced-fat cheddar. | Make your thickening paste by mixing Wondra flour with a little bit of milk, then whisk in the remaining milk called for in the recipe. |
| Cookies | Generally you can only cut the fat by half. If the original recipe calls for 1 cup of butter, for example, try cutting it to 1/2 a cup. | Fat-free cream cheese for rich cookies; some fruit purees may work in fruit drop cookies. Maple syrup for oatmeal cookies. |

# Ideal fat thresholds and fat replacements for different types of recipes (continued)

| Recipe | Fat Threshold | Fat Replacements |
|---|---|---|
| Frosting | | Cut the fat in half by using a high-quality diet margarine like I Can't Believe It's Not Butter Light. |
| Marinades | 1 tablespoon canola oil per cup of marinade (or none at all). | Fruit juices or beer to help balance the sharpness of the more acidic ingredients (vinegar, tomato juice). |
| Muffins and nut breads | 2 tablespoons canola oil for a 12-muffin recipe. | Fat-free sour cream, flavored yogurts, fruit purees, maple syrup. |
| Pie and other pastry crusts | 3 tablespoons shortening or canola margarine for every 1 cup flour. | Use fat-free cream cheese and substitute buttermilk for the required water. |
| Vinaigrette dressings | 1 to 2 tablespoons olive or canola oil per 1/2 cup dressing. | Fruit juice, fruit purees (raspberry or pear), light corn syrup, maple syrup, nonalcoholic wines (depending on the recipe). |
| White sauces and gravies | 1 teaspoon butter per serving of sauce. | Add a little more milk or broth to replace the lost fat. I use whole milk for a rich white sauce because, to me, whole milk *is* cream. |

### Fat-free, reduced-fat, or light mayonnaise

There are times when I might use reduced-fat mayonnaise in place of fats or oil, such as when I need something that will coat a food or help a crumb coating adhere. I also use it for thickening, for example, in a reduced-fat creamy salad dressing.

### Maple syrup

I have used maple syrup instead of lard in chicken sausages and in place of oil in spice cakes, quick breads, and certain types of cookies.

### Molasses

Substitute molasses for some meat marinades or sauces. Molasses can also be used as a replacement for some of the butter or oil in certain quick breads, coffee cakes, and spice cookies.

### Corn syrup

You can reduce the amount of sugar called for in baking recipes and then replace some of the fat with corn syrup. There's something about the chemical structure of corn syrup that makes it hold on to its moisture in a baked product longer. It releases moisture slowly, over time, into the food.

# Food Step 6: Avoid trouble spices

Some people with IBS tend not to tolerate hot sauce, spicy barbecue sauce, or foods that contain:

| | |
|---|---|
| chili powder | curry |
| hot chili peppers | ginger |
| garlic | |

You may tolerate these spices in small amounts, or it could be that not all of them cause problems for you. You might do just fine with curry, ginger, and garlic, but have trouble with chili peppers or chili powder.

Take heart though—there are ways to add flavor and spice to your dishes without precipitating IBS symptoms. Use the herbs and spices that tend not to be problematic, such as basil, oregano, thyme, and rosemary.

# Food Step 7: Avoid alcohol

Alcohol stimulates the digestive tract by getting digestive juices flowing, so it can cause heartburn, stomach pain, and diarrhea.

# Food Step 8: Avoid gassy foods

For some people with IBS, it isn't the gas that bothers them as much as the abdominal pain and bloating that tends to come with it. Reducing the amount of gassy foods in your diet may help relieve the symptoms of abdominal pain, gas, and bloating.

Many gassy foods contain carbohydrates, which are not completely digested in the small intestine. By the time they get to the end of the large intestine, bacteria (normally present in the intestines) has digested these carbohydrates and produced gas as a breakdown by-product. Which foods are we talking about (as if you don't already know)? Certain fruits and vegetables and dried beans and peas (and dairy for people who are lactose intolerant) are particular offenders.

- Raw vegetables (including cucumber and lettuce in salads).

- The following vegetables can cause trouble even when they are cooked:

| | | |
|---|---|---|
| broccoli | kohlrabi | rutabaga |
| brussels sprouts | leeks | sauerkraut |
| cabbage | onions | scallions |
| cauliflower | red/green peppers | shallots |
| cucumber | pimientos | turnips |
| corn | radishes | chili peppers |

- Dried peas, beans, and lentils including:

| | |
|---|---|
| black-eyed peas | navy beans |
| kidney beans | split peas |
| lima beans | lentils |

- The following fruits can cause trouble in some people:

| | |
|---|---|
| apples (with peel) | honeydew melon |
| avocados | prunes |
| cantaloupe | watermelon |

- Other food/drinks that may cause trouble:

beer

seeds (sesame, poppy, sunflower, flaxseed)

hard-boiled eggs

soft drinks

nuts

wheat germ

popcorn

spices (chili powder, garlic, hot sauce, curry, ginger, spicy BBQ sauce)

Some people with IBS may have a specific disturbance in bacterial fermentation and colonic gas production. Studies have found that gas production in the colon, particularly of hydrogen gas, is indeed greater in people with IBS compared to controls. One recent study put IBS gas sufferers on a standard exclusion diet. Beef and dairy were excluded (and replaced by soy products), cereals other than rice were excluded, and yeast, citrus fruits, and caffeinated drinks were restricted. The researchers concluded that gas production and symptoms were reduced.

# Food Step 9:
## Eat smaller, more frequent meals

Large meals can bring on cramping and diarrhea in people with IBS. Post-meal exacerbation of pain and other gastro-intestinal symptoms were seen in about half of a sample of patients with IBS (*American Journal of Medicine* 107).

By eating smaller meals and portions, but eating more often, we reduce the intestinal load at any one time. You are pacing the intestines, not giving them more than they can handle at any one time. When you think of it that way, it makes sense, doesn't it? Don't even think about skipping meals. Your bowel likes routine. It wants you to eat regular meals, which means not skipping meals if you can help it.

## Easier said than done

Our society is based on three meals a day (with dinner traditionally being the largest), so if you eat out often, you will find this food step particularly difficult. Restaurants tend to serve large portions and that's all there is to it. It requires extra diligence at restaurants to eat only half your meal and save the rest for later (or order less to begin with). If you are having spaghetti, for example, you could eat the salad and half your entrée, then have the bread and the rest of your spaghetti later or the next day. I'm not saying it isn't going to be difficult, but it can be done. If it helps minimize your symptoms, well worth it.

# Food Step 10: Exercise!

Exercise can be therapeutic for people with IBS. Certainly exercise helps those who tend to have bouts of constipation. This is because exercise is another intestinal stimulant. Moving around and using muscles seems to help get things moving in your gastrointestinal (GI) tract. It can also be helpful for the people with other IBS symptoms, because exercise is a powerful stress reducer. By exercising, you are helping to reduce the stress that could contribute to an IBS flare-up.

You might find that your body prefers to exercise at a certain time of day. Perhaps first thing in the morning works for you and seems to minimize constipation. Or, if your bowel is most active first thing in the morning, exercising later on might suit you better. Experiment with different times.

Another option is to exercise in short spurts throughout the day. For example, you could walk your dog in the morning and then ride your stationary bike while you watch a half-hour show in the evening. Or, if you work in an office, you can walk the long way from your car, the subway, or the bus station to your office and take the stairs a few times during the day. Then, maybe do a little something at home in the evening. Often we are most limited by our lifestyles and work schedules, so do what you can.

If you haven't been exercising on a regular basis, getting started is the hardest part. Once you get going though, and you start feeling the difference (more energy, less constipation, better sleep), it's easier to keep it up. If you are a self-described couch potato, then maybe riding a stationary bike while you watch TV is a good place to start. I personally find an hour goes by quickly when I'm watching one of my favorite shows atop my comfortable stationary bike. One of the keys to exercise success is finding types of exercise you actually enjoy doing and that fit into your lifestyle. Do this and you will be much more likely to stick to it.

 Chapter 5

# The 20 Recipes You Cannot Live Without

I hope you will enjoy the collection of recipes in this chapter. You will find recipes to boost your fiber (such as Raisin Bran Muffins) or work whole-wheat bread into your day (Snickerdoodle Toast), and recipes that go easy on the intestines (Crock-Pot Chicken Breasts, Salmon in. Wine Sauce, and Microwave Lemon Rice). But mostly you will find lower-fat recipes for the high-fat foods we know and love (burgers and fries, spinach manicotti with alfredo sauce, lasagna, chocolate cream cheese muffins, and more). That's my specialty.

**Please note:** The following is a key to the abbreviations used in the recipes: tablespoon (tbs.), teaspoon (tsp.), gram (g), milligram (mg), ounces (oz.), pound (lb.).

# Raisin Bran Muffins

These muffins are absolutely addictive. They freeze well, so they make a great breakfast on the run or a quick snack or dinner bread.

**Makes 18 muffins.**

- 1 cup whole-wheat flour
- 1 1/2 cup unbleached white flour
- 1 1/4 cup sugar
- 2 1/2 tsp. baking soda
- 1 tsp. salt
- 3 cups raisin bran cereal
- 2 cups low-fat buttermilk
- 1/4 cup canola oil
- 1/4 cup maple syrup
- 1 large egg
- 2 egg whites

1. Preheat oven to 425 degrees and line 18 muffin cups with papers (or coat with canola cooking spray).

2. Place flours, sugar, baking soda, and salt in large mixing bowl and beat on low speed of mixer to blend well. Add raisin bran and beat on low until blended.

3. Pour buttermilk, oil, maple syrup, and eggs into medium bowl and whisk with fork to blend well. Pour into dry ingredients and beat on low speed briefly just to blend.

4. Spoon 1/4 cup batter into each prepared muffin cup and bake until tester inserted in center of muffins comes out clean (approximately 15 minutes). Transfer to rack and cool.

*Note:* You can cover the mixing bowl and chill the muffin batter in the refrigerator for up to one week, although the mixture will thicken.

**Per muffin:** 197 calories, 4.5 g protein, 37 g carbohydrate, 4 g fat (.5 g saturated fat), 12 mg cholesterol, 3 g fiber, 370 mg sodium. Calories from fat: 18 percent.

# Blueberry Oat Bran Streusel Muffins

**Makes 12 muffins.**

**Struesel topping**

- 3 tbs. unbleached flour
- 3 tbs. sugar
- 1/2 tsp. ground cinnamon
- 2 tbs. canola margarine

**Blueberries**

- 1 1/2 cups fresh or frozen blueberries
- 1 to 2 tbs. flour (optional)

**Batter**

- 2/3 cup oat bran
- 1 1/3 cups unbleached flour
- 2 tsp. baking powder
- 1/2 tsp. salt
- 2 tbs. canola margarine
- 1/3 cup light corn syrup
- 1/3 cup granulated sugar
- 1 egg

- 2 egg whites (or 1/4 cup egg substitute)
- 1 tsp. vanilla extract
- 1/4 tsp. grated lemon peel (lemon zest)
- 1/2 cup milk (low-fat or whole)

1. Preheat oven to 375 degrees. Line 12 muffin cups with papers (or coat with canola cooking spray).

2. Make struesel topping: Place flour, sugar, and cinnamon in small bowl and blend well. Cut in margarine with fork until mixture resembles course crumbs; set aside.

3. Prepare blueberries: In small bowl sprinkle flour over blueberries if desired (to keep the blueberries from turning the batter purple); set aside.

4. Prepare batter: Combine oat bran, flour, baking powder, and salt in medium bowl.

5. In mixer bowl, beat margarine, corn syrup, and sugar at medium speed until light and fluffy. Add egg and egg whites, beating until smooth. Add vanilla and lemon peel.

6. On lowest speed beat in dry ingredients, alternating with the milk, just until blended (do not overmix). Fold blueberries into the batter gently.

7. Spoon 1/4 cup of batter into each muffin cup. Sprinkle with streusel topping. Bake approximately 20 minutes or until toothpick inserted in center of muffin comes out clean. Cool in pans on wire rack.

**Per serving** (made with low-fat milk): 186 calories, 4 g protein, 34 g carbohydrate, 4.9 g fat (.9 g saturated fat),

18 mg cholesterol, 2 g fiber, 233 mg sodium. Calories from fat: 23 percent.

*Note:* These muffins freeze well; reheat in microwave.

 # Pumpkin Pecan Wheat Bread

**Makes 10 slices.**

- 3/4 cup unbleached white flour
- 1/2 cup plus 2 tbs. whole-wheat flour
- 1 1/2 tsp. pumpkin pie spice
- 1 tsp. baking powder
- 1/2 tsp. baking soda
- 1/4 tsp. salt
- 1/4 cup finely chopped pecans
- 3 tbs. canola margarine or butter, softened
- 1/4 cup plus 1 tbs. light or fat-free cream cheese
- 1/2 cup granulated sugar
- 1/2 cup packed dark brown sugar
- 1 large egg
- 2 tbs. egg substitute or 1 egg white
- 1/2 cup solid-pack pumpkin
- 1 tsp. finely chopped orange zest
- 2 tbs. concentrated orange juice (or orange liqueur)

1. Preheat oven to 350 degrees. Coat an 8 1/2" x 4 1/2" loaf pan with canola cooking spray (or oil) and lightly flour.
2. Combine flours, pumpkin pie spice, baking powder, baking soda, salt, and pecans in medium bowl.

3. In a large bowl, using an electric mixer, cream the margarine or butter and cream cheese. Add the sugars and beat until light.

4. Add the egg and egg substitute or egg white and beat well.

5. Beat in pumpkin, orange zest, and orange juice.

6. Add the dry ingredients to the pumpkin mixture and mix just until blended. Spoon into prepared pan and smooth out top with spatula. Bake for approximately 45 minutes or until toothpick inserted in center comes out clean. Cool for 10 minutes. Remove from pan; cool completely on wire rack.

**Per serving:** 212 calories, 4.5 g protein, 32.5 g carbohydrate, 7.5 g fat (2 g saturated fat), 26 mg cholesterol, 2 g fiber, 235 mg sodium. Calories from fat: 32 percent.

 # Snickerdoodle Wheat Toast

If snickerdoodle cookies could be a breakfast bread, this would be it. Whole-wheat bread gives this breakfast treat a shot of fiber, and canola margarine keeps it tasting buttery without all the saturated fat.

**Makes 5 snickerdoodle toasts.**

- 2 tbs. canola margarine (butter or another margarine can be used)
- 3 tsp. granulated sugar
- 3/4 tsp. ground cinnamon
- 5 slices whole-wheat bread (about 40 grams each)

1. Place margarine, sugar, and cinnamon into a custard cup or similar. Blend with a fork or spoon

until ingredients are completely mixed and a spread is formed.

2. Toast bread and spread it with the snickerdoodle mixture.

**Per snickerdoodle toast:** 150 calories, 4 g protein, 21 g carbohydrate, 6 g fat (.8 g saturated fat), 0 mg cholesterol, 2.5 g fiber, 254 mg sodium. Calories from fat: 35 percent.

 # Wheat Focaccia with Tomato and Cheese

At first glance it looks like this recipe takes a long time to make, but it actually goes very quickly—and you don't even need a bread machine! Served with soup and vegetables, this pizza-like bread makes a light meal.

**Makes 12 servings.**

- 2 tbs. extra-virgin olive oil
- 2 cloves garlic, minced or pressed (omit if you have trouble with garlic)

**Dough:**

- 1 3/4 cups warm water (110 to 115 degrees)
- 1 tbs. sugar
- 1 package (1 tablespoon) rapid-rise yeast
- 2 1/2 cups whole-wheat flour
- 2 1/2 cups unbleached white flour
- 2 tbs. extra virgin olive oil
- 1 tsp. salt

**Topping and prep:**

- Olive or canola cooking spray
- 1/3 cup shredded Parmesan cheese
- 3/4 tsp. dried oregano

- 1/4 to 1/2 tsp. salt
- 2/3 cup bottled marinara sauce
- 4 oz. part-skim mozzarella cheese, grated (1 cup packed)

1. Combine the 2 tablespoons oil and garlic in a small cup and set aside. (If possible, allow the oil to steep overnight before using.)

2. In medium bowl, combine the water, sugar, and yeast and gently stir until yeast is dissolved. Let stand 5 minutes or until foamy.

3. Stir 1 cup of the flour into the yeast mixture, then stir in the oil and salt. Stir in remaining flour. Knead briefly on a floured surface to incorporate the flour.

4. Let the dough rest approximately 10 minutes while you preheat the oven to 450 degrees and prepare the pan (generously coat a 13" x 9" baking pan with cooking spray).

5. Turn the dough into the pan and pat out evenly with your fingertips. Flour your fingertips and make indentations in the surface of the dough at 1-inch intervals. Spread the garlic-oil mixture evenly over the dough with your fingertips.

6. In a small bowl, stir together the Parmesan cheese, oregano, and salt (or combine in a mini-food processor). Sprinkle the dough with the cheese mixture. Bake for 15 to 20 minutes or until the top is nicely browned. Turn the oven off. Spread the marinara sauce evenly over the focaccia. Top with mozzarella cheese and put it back in the warm oven until the cheese is melted (approximately 3 minutes). Cut into rectangles and serve warm.

**Per serving:** 274 calories, 10.3 g protein, 41.3 g carbohydrate, 8 g fat (2.4 g saturated fat), 7 mg cholesterol, 4 g fiber, 413 mg sodium. Calories from fat: 26 percent.

 # Hero Sandwiches with Reduced-Fat Russian Dressing

**Makes 3 sandwiches.**

- 6 large slices whole-wheat bread (half of a one-pound loaf of unsliced French bread can also be used)
- 3 tbs. Russian dressing (recipe on page 79)
- 2 tbs. chopped green onion (optional)
- 1/2 cucumber, sliced (optional)
- 6 ounces sliced premium very lean ham
- 4 ounces sliced reduced-fat Swiss or light Jarlsberg cheese
- 1 tomato, sliced

1. With a bread knife, cut the bread horizontally in half. In a small bowl, mix the Russian dressing with the chopped green onion.
2. On the bottom of 3 slices of bread, layer the cucumber slices, ham, cheese, and tomato.
3. Spread the Russian dressing generously on top. Replace the top of bread. Slice into equal pieces to serve.

**Per serving (using whole-wheat bread):** 454 calories, 31 g protein, 50.5 g carbohydrate, 15.5 g fat (6 g saturated fat), 48 mg cholesterol, 6.3 g fiber, 1,600 mg sodium. Calories from fat: 30 percent.

**Russian Dressing**

**Makes 5 tablespoons.**

- 1 tbs. canola mayonnaise
- 1 tbs. light or fat-free sour cream
- 2 tbs. catsup
- 1/4 tsp. hot sauce or chili sauce
- 1 tsp. sugar
- 1 1/2 tsp. seasoned rice vinegar, white wine vinegar, or white vinegar
- 1 tsp. lemon juice
- 1/4 tsp. Worcestershire sauce
- 1/8 tsp. salt
- a pinch or two of freshly ground pepper

Combine all ingredients in a small bowl; stir well to blend. The dressing can be stored, covered, in the refrigerator for up to two weeks; stir before serving.

#  Reduced-Fat Burger and Fries

To time your cooking so the burger and fries are done at the same time, preheat the oven for the fries, then mix up the burger mixture and press into patties. Start cooking the fries, then proceed to the burgers.

**Makes 4 servings.**

**Burgers:**

- 1 lb. ground sirloin or any extra-lean ground beef
- 2 tbs. bottled steak sauce
- 1/4 to 1/2 cup finely chopped onion (optional)

- 1/4 cup egg substitute or 1 beaten egg
- freshly ground black pepper
- garlic salt
- canola cooking spray
- 4 hamburger buns
- optional toppings: 4 thin slices reduced-fat cheese (sharp cheddar or Monterey Jack), catsup, mustard, lettuce, and sliced tomato.

1. In a large bowl, mix together ground beef, steak sauce, egg substitute, and onion, if desired.

2. Divide mixture into four portions and shape into 1/2"-thick patties.

3. Lightly sprinkle pepper and garlic salt on both sides of each burger.

4. Spray grill rack or pan with canola cooking spray. Grill the burgers over a medium flame or pan-fry over medium heat in a nonstick frying pan for about 5 minutes on each side or until they're cooked through.

5. If you like, top burgers with cheese in the final 30 seconds of cooking.

6. Serve the burgers on toasted buns and top as desired.

**Fries:**

- 12 oz. Ore Ida Country Style French Fries (frozen)

1. Preheat oven to 450 degrees.

2. Arrange frozen fries in a single layer on a thick baking sheet.

3. Bake in center of oven for approximately 15 to 20 minutes or until desired color and crispness.

**Per serving (burger and fries):** 422 calories, 25 g protein, 43.5 g carbohydrate, 16 g fat (5 g saturated fat), 31 mg cholesterol, 2.3 g fiber, 697 mg sodium. Calories from fat: 34 percent.

*Note:* If you use a whole-wheat bun or whole-wheat bread, the fiber will increase by about 4 grams a serving.

 # Spinach Ricotta Manicotti with Alfredo Sauce

**Makes 4 to 5 dinner entrees.**

**Alfredo sauce:**

- 1 tbs. butter
- 2 cups whole milk, divided use (fat-free half-and-half can also be used)
- 4 tbs. Wondra flour
- 1/8 tsp. nutmeg
- 1/8 tsp. white pepper
- 1/4 cup shredded Parmesan cheese

Melt butter in medium saucepan or microwave-safe medium bowl. Stir in 1/4 cup of the milk, flour, nutmeg, and pepper. Slowly stir in remaining milk. Cook on high in microwave (stirring every 2 minutes) or over medium-low heat on the stove (stirring constantly) until sauce thickens slightly. This will take approximately 10 to 14 minutes in the microwave and approximately 3 or 4 minutes on the stove. Stir in Parmesan cheese.

**Manicotti:**

- 10-oz. box frozen, chopped spinach
- 15-oz. container part-skim ricotta cheese

- 3/4 cup freshly grated Parmesan cheese
- 1/2 cup egg substitute
- 4 tbs. minced fresh parsley leaves (preferably flat leaf)
- salt and pepper to taste
- 8 to 10 manicotti shells cooked according to package directions
- 8 to 10 thin slices proscuitto (approx. 3 oz.)
- 2 cups Alfredo sauce

1. Preheat oven to 350 degrees. Coat a 9" x 13" baking pan with canola cooking spray.
2. Place spinach, ricotta, Parmesan, egg substitute, and parsley to mixing bowl and beat on low to blend well. Add salt and pepper to taste.
3. Fill each cooled manicotti shell with approximately 1/3 cup of the filling. Place in the prepared pan and lay a slice of prosciutto over each.
4. Pour Alfredo sauce evenly over manicotti. Bake in middle of oven approximately 30 minutes. Let stand 10 minutes before serving.

**Per serving (if 5 servings per recipe):** 454 calories, 30.5 g protein, 43.5 g carbohydrate, 17.5 g fat (10 g saturated fat), 55 mg cholesterol, 2.5 g fiber, 642 mg sodium. Calories from fat: 35 percent.

*Note:* The original recipe contains 620 calories, 36 grams fat (21 grams saturated fat), and 190 mg cholesterol per serving.

 ## Chicken Parmigiana

Chicken Parmigiana is one of my favorite restaurant entrees. This recipe is much lower in fat and will hopefully work better for you than the restaurant version.

**Makes 4 servings.**

- 1/2 cup egg substitute
- 3/4 cup Italian-style or plain bread crumbs
- 1/8 tsp. freshly ground pepper
- 4 boneless, skinless chicken breasts, pounded well with a meat mallet to even the thickness
- olive or canola cooking spray
- 2 tsp. olive or canola oil
- 1 1/2 cups bottled marinara sauce
- 3/4 cup grated part-skim mozzarella cheese (or 3 oz. thinly sliced)
- 2 to 3 tbs. grated Parmesan cheese

1. Put the egg substitute in a pie plate. On waxed paper, blend the bread crumbs with the pepper. Dip the chicken breasts first in the egg then in the bread crumbs, then repeat to coat well. Set each piece of chicken aside on a plate.

2. Coat a large heavy nonstick skillet generously with cooking spray. Add the oil and heat over medium-high heat until hot. Add the chicken and brown on the bottom, approximately five minutes. Spray the tops of the chicken with cooking spray, flip over, and brown on the second side, approximately 5 minutes.

3. When the chicken is brown on both sides, spoon the sauce over each breast, top with the mozzarella, and sprinkle with the Parmesan. Reduce the heat to low, cover and continue cooking for approximately 3 to 5 minutes, or until the cheese is melted.

**Per serving:** 394 calories, 41 g protein, 25 g carbohydrate, 14 g fat (4.7 g saturated fat), 87 mg cholesterol, 1 g fiber, 600–1,000 mg sodium. Calories from fat: 33 percent.

*Note:* The original recipe (using veal) contains 669 calories, 250 mg cholesterol, and 41 g fat!

 ## Country Pot Roast

### Makes at least 6 servings.

- 3- to 5-lb. center-cut cross-rib (shoulder) roast, trimmed of visible fat
- 1/4 cup unbleached white flour
- 1 1/2 tsp. canola oil
- 1 cup tomato juice, tomato sauce, or bottled marinara sauce
- 3 garlic cloves, minced (omit if you have a problem with garlic)
- 4 carrots, sliced
- 3 large potatoes, quartered
- 1 large onion, coarsely chopped (omit if you have a problem with onion)
- 1 cup sliced celery
- 1 tsp. salt
- 1 1/2 tsp. dried oregano
- 1/4 tsp. freshly ground pepper

1. Place the roast on a cutting board or waxed paper and coat with the flour.
2. Heat the oil in a Dutch oven or large saucepan over medium-high heat. Add the roast and cook until browned on all sides.
3. Add all the remaining ingredients and bring to a boil. Reduce heat to low, cover pot, and simmer for 2 to 4 hours, depending on the size of the roast, or until the meat is fork-tender, turning several times.

4. Transfer meat to a cutting board. In batches, puree the cooking liquid and vegetables in a blender at high speed. Pour back into the pan or into a serving bowl. Slice the roast and serve with the vegetable gravy.

**Per serving:** 405 calories, 37 g protein, 39.5 g carbohydrate, 13 g fat (5 g saturated fat), 90 mg cholesterol, 5 g fiber, 606 mg sodium. Calories from fat: 29 percent.

*Note:* Standard pot roast recipes contain more than 600 calories and 38 grams of fat per serving!

 # Crock-Pot Spaghetti

This is a family favorite. We make it every single week.
**Makes 4 servings.**

- canola cooking spray
- 1 lb. ground sirloin or other extra-lean ground beef
- 25-oz. bottle marinara sauce (about 2 3/4 cups)
- 4 garlic cloves, minced or pressed (omit if garlic isn't well tolerated)
- 1 onion, chopped (omit if onion isn't well tolerated)
- 4 to 6 cups cooked spaghetti

1. Coat a large, nonstick frying pan with canola cooking spray. Set heat to medium. Add ground sirloin, breaking it up into small pieces with spatula. Cook, stirring occasionally, until nicely browned. Place in Crock-Pot.

2. Pour marinara sauce into Crock-Pot. Add garlic and/or onion, as desired. Stir well to blend.

3. Cover, turn Crock-Pot to low and cook approximately 8 to 10 hours (3 hours on high).

4. Stir spaghetti noodles into Crock-Pot, or spoon each serving of sauce over a serving of cooked noodles.

**Per serving:** 421 calories, 32.5 g protein, 55 g carbohydrate, 8 g fat (3 g saturated fat), 69 mg cholesterol, 3.5 g fiber, 800 mg sodium. Calories from fat: 17 percent.

 # Mini Meatloaf Au Gratin

Many meatloaf recipes can cause problems because they are often high in fat (some contain sausage meat), or spicy, or both. This recipe is a mild but flavorful version of this American classic. You can freeze the loaves and pull them out when you need a quick dinner for one or two. **Makes 5 mini loaves.**

- 5 aluminum mini loaf pans (3 1/2" x 6")— available in most supermarkets
- 2 lb. ground sirloin or other extra-lean ground beef
- 1/4 cup egg substitute
- 3/4 cup reduced-fat sharp cheddar cheese
- 1 small onion, chopped (omit if onion causes you trouble)
- 1/3 cup plain bread crumbs
- 1 1/2 tbs. Worchestershire sauce
- 1 tbs. Dijon or prepared mustard
- 1/2 tsp. salt
- 1/2 tsp. pepper
- 1 1/4 cup tomato sauce

1. Preheat oven to 350 degrees. Coat 5 mini loaf pans with canola cooking spray.

2. Add ground beef, egg substitute, cheese, onion, bread crumbs, Worchestershire sauce, mustard, salt, and pepper to large bowl. Mix well with hands or wooden spoon.

3. Add approximately 1 cup of the mixture to each prepared loaf pan. Bake about 25 minutes. Pour approximately 1/4 cup of tomato sauce over each mini loaf while in pan and bake an additional 5 to 8 minutes to heat tomato sauce.

*Serving suggestion:* Serve each mini meatloaf with 1/2 cup of steamed rice and 1/2 cup of peas and carrots.

**Per serving (just meatloaf):** 339 calories, 36 g protein, 12 g carbohydrate, 15.5 g fat (6.8 g saturated fat), 58 mg cholesterol, 1.6 g fiber, 815 mg sodium. Calories from fat: 43 percent.

**Per serving (when served with rice, peas, and carrots):** 517 calories, 41 g protein, 50 g carbohydrate, 16 g fat (7 g saturated fat), 58 mg cholesterol, 5 g fiber, 882 mg sodium. Calories from fat: 29 percent.

 # Quick & Mild (No-Boil) Lasagna

Here is a low-fat, quick, mild recipe for no-boil lasagna. It's a favorite in my house.

**Makes 8 servings.**

- 3/4 lb. ground sirloin or other extra-lean ground beef
- 26-oz. jar of marinara (or spaghetti) sauce with 2 g of fat per serving
- 14 1/2-oz. can of vegetable or chicken broth
- 15-oz. container part-skim or low-fat ricotta cheese

- 1 cup grated part-skim mozzarella cheese
- 5 tbs. grated Parmesan cheese
- 3 tbs. chopped fresh parsley or 1 tbs. dried parsley
- 3 tbs. chopped fresh basil leaves (optional)
- 1/4 cup egg substitute
- 1/2 tsp. salt (optional)
- 1/4 tsp. pepper
- 9 wide lasagna noodles (uncooked), about 9.6 oz.

1. Preheat oven to 350 degrees. In large, nonstick saucepan, brown ground sirloin well. Stir in marinara sauce and broth and set aside.
2. In medium bowl, combine ricotta, 3/4 cup of the mozzarella, 3 tablespoons Parmesan cheese, parsley, basil, egg substitute, salt, and pepper.
3. In 13" x 9" baking dish, layer 1 1/2 cups meat sauce and then 3 strips of uncooked noodles. Dot the noodles with 1/3 of the cheese mixture. Cover the cheese with 1 1/2 cups meat sauce and 3 more strips of noodles. Dot the noodles with another third of the cheese mixture. Top the cheese with 1 1/2 cups meat sauce and the last 3 noodles. Dot the noodles with the remaining cheese mixture and meat sauce. Sprinkle the remaining 2 tablespoons Parmesan and 1/4 cup mozzarella over the top.
4. Spray one side of foil with canola cooking spray (so the cheese doesn't stick) and cover the lasagna tightly. Bake for 35 minutes. Uncover the lasagna and bake 15 more minutes. Let stand 10 minutes.

**Per serving:** 346 calories, 24 g protein, 34.5 g carbohydrate, 12 g fat (6 g saturated fat), 38 mg cholesterol, 3 g fiber, 935 mg sodium. Calories from fat: 31 percent.

# Classic Oatmeal-Raisin Cookies

Chocolate can give some people with IBS trouble, and so can high-fat treats. This reduced-fat version of classic oatmeal-raisin cookies, with half the fat and 28 percent fewer calories than the original, is a great, chewy alternative to chocolate chip cookies.

**Makes about 32 large cookies.**

- 1/4 cup plus 1/8 cup canola margarine or butter, softened (margarine must have 11 grams of fat per tablespoon to work the same as butter in this recipe)
- 1/4 cup plus 1/8 cup fat-free or light cream cheese
- 1 cup packed brown sugar
- 1/2 cup sugar
- 1/4 cup low-fat buttermilk
- 1/4 cup egg substitute
- 2 tbs. maple syrup
- 2 tsp. vanilla extract
- 1 cup unbleached white flour
- 1/2 tsp. baking soda
- 1 1/2 tsp. ground cinnamon
- 1/4 tsp. salt
- 3 cups quick or old-fashioned oats
- 1 cup raisins
- 1/2 cup chopped walnuts (optional)

1. Preheat oven to 350 degrees. Coat two thick cookie sheets or baking stones with canola cooking spray.

2 In a large bowl, beat the butter with the cream cheese. Beat in the sugars, buttermilk, egg substitute, maple syrup, and vanilla, and beat until light and fluffy.

3. Combine the flour, baking soda, cinnamon, and salt; beat into the butter mixture, mixing well. Stir in the oats, raisins, and nuts, mixing well.

4. Drop spoonfuls of dough 2 inches apart on the prepared cookie sheets.

5. Bake one cookie sheet at a time in the upper third of the oven for approximately 10 minutes, or until lightly browned. Transfer the cookies to wire racks to cool completely. Store in airtight container.

**Per cookie:** 115 calories, 2.5 g protein, 21 g carbohydrate, 2.7 g fat (.4 g saturated fat), .3 mg cholesterol, 1.2 g fiber, 77 mg sodium. Calories from fat: 21 percent.

 # Black-Bottom Cupcakes/ Muffins

This is a reduced-fat version of the popular black-bottom cupcakes/muffins. Although the chocolate and fat is scaled down, these muffins are still totally addicting and delicious. These muffins are great when you need a quick chocolate fix.

**Makes 18 cupcakes.**

**Cream cheese filling:**

- 3/4 cup neufchatel or light cream cheese, softened (fat-free can also be used)
- 1 tsp. vanilla extract
- 1/3 cup plus 1 tbs. sugar
- 1 large egg

**Muffin batter:**

- 1 1/2 cups unbleached white flour
- 1 cup sugar
- 1/4 cup unsweetened cocoa

- 1 tsp. baking soda
- 1/2 tsp. salt
- 1 cup water
- 2 tbs. canola oil
- 3 tbs. light or fat-free sour cream
- 1 tbs. white vinegar
- 1 1/2 tsp. vanilla extract
- 1/3 cup chopped almonds (optional)
- 2 tbs. sugar (optional)

1. Preheat oven to 350 degrees. Line 18 muffin cups with paper cups.
2. Make cream cheese filling by beating the ingredients together in a small bowl until smooth; set aside.
3. In a large bowl, combine the flour, sugar, cocoa, baking soda, and salt; mix well. Add the water, oil, sour cream, vinegar, and vanilla. Using an electric mixer, beat for 2 minutes on medium speed.
4. Fill the muffin cups half-full with the batter. Top each with a tablespoon of the cream cheese mixture. Sprinkle chopped almonds and sugar over the top if desired.
5. Bake for 20 minutes, or until the cream cheese mixture is light golden brown. Cool for 15 minutes; remove from the pans. Cool completely. Store in the refrigerator.

**Per serving:** 143 calories, 3 g protein, 25 g carbohydrate, 3.7 g fat (1.5 g saturated fat), 17 mg cholesterol, 1 g fiber, 185 mg sodium. Calories from fat: 23 percent.

*Note:* Original recipe contains 250 calories, 25 mg cholesterol, and 13 grams of fat per serving.

# Microwave Lemon Rice

**Makes 4 servings.**

- 1 1/2 cups unrinsed Basmati rice
- 2 1/4 cups chicken broth
- 2 to 3 tbs. lemon juice
- 2/3 cup frozen petite green peas (if tolerated)
- salt and pepper to taste

1. Place rice, broth, and lemon juice in 2- or 3-quart microwave-safe dish and cook on high, uncovered, approximately 15 to 17 minutes, or until steam holes appear in rice.
2. Sprinkle peas over rice, cover dish, and cook on high approximately 5 to 7 minutes or until rice is fully cooked and peas are lightly cooked.
3. Fluff with fork and serve.

**Per serving:** 296 calories, 9 g protein, 60 g carbohydrate, 1.3 g fat (.4 g saturated fat), 0 mg cholesterol, 2 g fiber, 460 mg sodium. Calories from fat: 4 percent.

 # Microwave Orange Tapioca Pudding

If you don't care for orange, then try lemon curd or apple butter with the tapioca instead.

**Makes 6 servings.**

- 1/4 cup sugar
- 3 tbs. Minute tapioca
- 2 3/4 cups milk (low-fat or whole, whichever is better tolerated)
- 1/4 cup egg substitute

- 2 tbs. orange marmalade (lemon curd or apple butter can be substituted)
- 1 tsp. vanilla

1. Mix sugar, tapioca, milk, egg, and marmalade in microwavable bowl. Microwave on high 10 to 12 minutes until mixture comes to a full boil, stirring every 2 minutes.
2. Stir in vanilla. Cool 20 minutes; stir. Spoon into serving dishes. Serve warm or chilled. Store in refrigerator.

**Per serving:** 127 calories, 5 g protein, 22.5 g carbohydrate, 2 g fat (1.3 g saturated fat), 8 mg cholesterol, 0 g fiber, 73 mg sodium. Calories from fat: 14 percent.

#  Turkey Teriyaki Burger

**Makes 6 burgers.**

- 1 lb. ground turkey
- 1 cup steamed rice (leftover rice works fine)
- 1/2 tsp. chopped or minced ginger (omit if you don't tolerate ginger well)
- 1/4 cup teriyaki sauce
- canola cooking spray
- 6 sesame seed buns
- optional toppings: soy sauce or sweet and sour sauce, lettuce, and tomato slices

1. Place turkey, rice, ginger, and teriyaki sauce in large bowl; blend well using a spoon or your hands.
2. Divide mixture evenly into 6 portions. Form into 1/2"-thick burgers.

3. Spray grill rack or nonstick skillet with cooking spray. Grill or pan-fry over medium heat. Cook about 4 minutes on each side, or until nicely browned and cooked through.

**Per serving:** 279 calories, 16 g protein, 34 g carbohydrate, 8.3 g fat (2.5 g saturated), 46 mg cholesterol, 1.3 g fiber, 780 mg sodium. Calories from fat: 27 percent.

*Note:* If you use a whole-wheat bun or whole-wheat bread, the fiber will increase by approximately 4 grams per serving.

 # Crock-Pot Chicken Breasts

**Makes 6 servings.**

- 6 boneless, skinless chicken breasts (6 boneless, center-cut pork loin chops, trimmed of fat, can also be used)
- 1/2 cup flour
- 1 1/2 tsp. garlic salt
- 1 tsp. dry mustard
- 1 tbs. canola oil
- 6 carrots, cut into 1/4" slices
- 10 3/4-oz. can Campbell's Healthy Request Chicken and Rice Soup
- about 4 1/2 cups steamed rice

1. Spray bottom of Crock-Pot with canola cooking spray.

2. Mix flour, garlic salt, and dry mustard in medium-sized bowl. Dredge chicken (or pork chops) in flour mixture.

3. Add oil to large nonstick frying pan or skillet. Over medium heat, brown chicken breasts (or

chops) on both sides; place in Crock-Pot. Cover meat with sliced carrots. Add soup.

4. Cover and cook on low 8 hours.

5. Serve each chicken breast (or chop) over a mound of steamed rice. With slotted spoon, scoop out carrots and serve next to meat. Drizzle gravy over chicken (or chop).

**Per serving:** 444 calories, 35 g protein, 61.5 g carbohydrate, 5 g fat (1 g saturated fat), 71 mg cholesterol, 3.5 g fiber, 706 mg sodium. Calories from fat: 11 percent.

*Note:* Fiber increases to 5 grams per serving when brown rice is used.

# Microwaved Salmon in Wine Sauce

**Makes 2 or 3 servings**

- 1 1/2 tsp. olive oil
- 2 6-oz.or 3 4-oz. center-cut salmon fillets (about 1 1/2" thick at thickest part, skin and bones removed)
- 2 tbs. dry white wine
- 1 tbs. finely chopped fresh parsley
- 1 tsp. fresh, dried, or frozen chives (optional)
- garlic salt to taste
- freshly ground black pepper to taste

**Suggested side dishes:**

- 3 cups steamed rice or cooked noodles
- 3 cups steamed vegetables of your choice

1. Coat a square, microwave-safe, covered casserole dish with canola cooking spray. Place the salmon pieces in dish, folding the thin sides under if necessary so the fillets are of even thickness. Drizzle the wine

and olive oil over the salmon and sprinkle parsley, chives, garlic salt, and pepper over the top. Cover the casserole (or use microwave-safe plastic wrap to cover dish).

2. Microwave on high for 6 minutes. If your microwave does not have a turntable, turn the casserole a quarter turn every 2 minutes so the fish cooks evenly. Take the casserole dish out and let it stand a few minutes (without uncovering).

3. Test the salmon in the thickest part with a fork. If it isn't cooked throughout, heat another minute or two until done. Serve each salmon fillet on a mound of rice and spoon the wine sauce (the sauce in the bottom of the dish) over the top.

**Per serving (including rice and a green vegetable):** if 3 servings per recipe: 498 calories, 33 g protein, 66 g carbohydrate, 10.5 g fat (1.4 g saturated fat), 62 mg cholesterol, 6 g fiber, 100 mg sodium. Calories from fat: 19 percent.

# Chapter 6

# Navigating the Supermarket

**E**very time you set foot in a supermarket you are hit with hundreds of advertising claims: "Fat Free," "No Cholesterol," "Multigrain," "Baked Not Fried." They are designed to entice you. Remember: All these companies are trying to sell you something. They all want a piece of the food dollar pie. So don't be fooled—find out for yourself. *Read the nutrition label.* Nutrition labels don't lie.

Some breads boast that they are "multigrain" or "seven grain," but their nutrition labels show they have only one little gram of fiber per serving. Some "wheat" or "multigrain" crackers don't even have one gram of fiber per serving.

Generally, the more you know about a food product, the better off you'll be. What should you be looking for on the label? Start with the portion size. Remember, what the manufacturer thinks is a portion and what you think is a portion could be two very different things. Some products within the same category may even have different serving sizes. For example, some bread labels give the nutrition information for one slice, others for two slices. Some canned baked beans and chili give the nutrition information for a half cup, others for one cup. A serving of cereal can be anything from a half cup to one and a quarter cups, depending on which you choose.

Once you've mastered that, it's a good idea to get a quick sense of the product's:

- Calories.
- Fat grams.
- Saturated fat grams.
- Fiber grams.

That's what the rest of this chapter is here to help you with. We'll be taking a virtual tour of the typical supermarket, noting the calories, fat grams, fiber content, and more for different foods in order to help you master the 10 Food Steps to Freedom. We'll be examining the fiber contents of breads and cereals. We'll be looking at the better-tasting reduced-fat products available in every aisle of the supermarket. So, are you ready? Here we go.

# Looking for fiber in all the right places

Does it really matter which breads or cereals contain the most fiber? You bet it does. Think about it. Most people have a sandwich and a bowl of cereal almost every day. If the bread you make your sandwich with contains seven grams of fiber instead of two, and the bowl of cereal you eat has eight grams of fiber instead of two, it can really make a difference day after day. We are talking about getting 15 grams of fiber—instead of four—with just those two foods.

That's a difference of 11 grams, just like that! So we'll start with the breads and cereals with the most fiber and go from there.

# Whole-wheat breads and bagels

Many breads that seem like they would have tons of fiber, like multigrain ones, don't. You'd think that with all those grains going in, they should be able to squeeze out a couple of grams of fiber per slice. There are a few breads that have more fiber than that, and you might be surprised to see which ones those are (I know I was). The bottom line is that you have to check the labels of the breads you like to see just how much fiber they really have. The tricky part is that there are a few breads that list the grams of fiber per two slices, and the rest list it per one slice.

I spent an hour doing research in the bread aisle, and if a bread had less than 2 grams of fiber per slice it didn't make my clipboard. You can see the results on page 100.

# High-fiber cereals

If you eat a breakfast cereal a few times a week, you sit down to about 156 bowls of cereal a year. So whether you choose a whole-grain cereal can make a big difference in the amount of fiber you are eating. I'll tell you a secret: What really distinguishes one cereal from another is not its fat and sodium content, it's the sugar and fiber.

The cereals that have a lot more sugar are usually the ones that have a lot less fiber, too. The table on page 101 lists most of the cereals that have five grams of fiber or more per serving. Notice that Cheerios and Whole Grain Wheaties didn't make the cut.

## Whole-Wheat Breads and Bagels

| | Fiber(g) | Fat(g) | Calories |
|---|---|---|---|
| **Breads (per slice)** | | | |
| **EarthGrains:** | | | |
| Country Hearth 100% Whole Wheat | 3 | 110 | 1.5 |
| Iron Kids | 2 | 80 | 1 |
| **Mrs. Wright's:** | | | |
| 100% Whole Wheat | 2 | 70 | 1 |
| Wheat Bread | 2 | 70 | 1 |
| Winner's Special Recipe Bread | 2 | 70 | 1 |
| **Northwest Grain Country:** | | | |
| 100% Whole Wheat | 3 | 100 | 1.5 |
| Early American | 2 | 110 | 1 |
| **Oregon Bread:** | | | |
| Whole Wheat Hazelnut | 3 | 140 | 4.5 |
| Western Hazelnut | 2 | 130 | 4.5 |
| **Oroweat:** | | | |
| Light 100% Whole Wheat | 3.5 | 40 | 0.25 |
| Light Country Potato Bread | 3 | 40 | 0.25 |
| Light Country Oat Bread | 2.5 | 40 | 0.5 |
| Light 9-Grain | 2.5 | 40 | 0.25 |
| 100% Whole Wheat | 2 | 90 | 1 |
| Health Nut | 2 | 100 | 2 |
| Branola | 2 | 90 | 1 |
| Honey Wheat Berry | 2 | 90 | 1 |
| Best Winter Wheat | 2 | 90 | 3 |
| **Roman Meal:** | | | |
| Sun Grain Bread | 2 | 100 | 2 |
| Dakota Wheat Bread | 2 | 90 | 1 |
| **Wonder:** | | | |
| Light Wheat | 2.5 | 40 | 0.25 |
| **Bagels (per bagel)** | | | |
| **Oroweat:** | | | |
| 100% Whole Wheat | 9 | 240 | 1.5 |
| Health Nut | 5 | 270 | 4.5 |
| Oat Nut | 4 | 270 | 4 |
| Multi Grain | 4 | 260 | 1.5 |
| **Sara Lee:** | | | |
| Honey Wheat | 4 | 250 | 1 |

## High-Fiber Cereals

| | Fiber(g) | Fat (g) | Calories |
|---|---|---|---|
| All-Bran Extra Fiber, 1/2 cup | 13 | 1 | 50 |
| Fiber One, 1/2 cup | 13 | 1 | 60 |
| All-Bran Original, 1/2 cup | 10 | 1 | 80 |
| 100% Bran, 1/3 cup | 8 | 0.5 | 80 |
| Kellogg's Raisin Bran, 1 cup | 8 | 1.5 | 200 |
| Post Raisin Bran, 1 cup | 8 | 1 | 190 |
| Shredded Wheat 'n Bran, 1 1/4 cup | 8 | 1 | 200 |
| Bite Size Frosted Mini-Wheats, 1 cup | 6 | 1 | 200 |
| Cracklin Oat Bran, 3/4 cup | 6 | 7 | 190 |
| Raisin Bran Crunch, 1 1/4 cup | 5 | 1 | 210 |
| Total Raisin Bran, 1 cup | 5 | 1 | 180 |
| Bran Flakes, 3/4 cup | 5 | 0.5 | 100 |
| Complete Wheat Bran Flakes, 3/4 cup | 5 | 0.5 | 90 |
| Crunchy Corn Bran, 3/4 cup | 5 | 1 | 90 |
| Spoon Size Shredded Wheat, 1 cup | 5 | 0.5 | 170 |
| Mini-Wheats (Raisin), 3/4 cup | 5 | 1 | 180 |
| Frosted Shredded Wheat, 1 cup | 5 | 1 | 190 |
| 100% Whole Grain Wheat Chex, 1 cup | 5 | 1.5 | 180 |
| Fruit & Fibre (Dates, Raisins, and Walnuts), 1 cup | 5 | 3 | 210 |
| Grape Nuts, 1/2 cup | 5 | 1 | 210 |
| Raisin Nut Bran, 3/4 cup | 5 | 4 | 200 |

# Frozen waffles

There are four Eggo waffles that contribute at least a fair amount of fiber. Topped with some fresh fruit and a drizzle of berry syrup, they're not a bad choice on a busy weekday morning.

## Frozen Waffles (2 per serving)

| | Cal. | Fiber[g] | Fat[g] (sat. fat) |
|---|---|---|---|
| Eggo Nutri-Grain Multigrain | 160 | 5 | 5(1) |
| Eggo Nutri-Grain Whole Wheat | 170 | 3 | 5(1) |
| Eggo Golden Oat | 140 | 3 | 2.5(.5) |
| Eggo Raisin & Bran | 210 | 5 | 6(0) |

# Beans: a little goes a long way

Some of you might think there is no way you can handle a serving of beans. Maybe you noticed some IBS symptoms after a big bowl of chili. But was it the beans in the chili, the fatty meat in the chili, or the spices? Or was it the fact that you had a bowl of chili instead of a cup?

Beans are a quick way to boost your fiber, with half a cup contributing around 6 grams of fiber. What's more, beans contain both types of fiber, soluble and insoluble. Try a small serving of beans, preferably not in a very fatty or spicy dish, so you can see how you do with just the beans. A bean burrito, either take-out or homemade, might be a good first bet (try low-fat pintos or refried beans with a flour tortilla, a sprinkling of cheese, and mild sauce).

Here are some of the canned bean products I found in my supermarket:

## Canned Bean Products (1/2 cup)

|  | Fiber (g) | Cal. | Fat(g) | Sod.(mg) |
|---|---|---|---|---|
| Taco Bell Vegetarian Refried | 8 | 140 | 2.5 | 500 |
| Ortega Refried Beans | 9 | 130 | 2.5 | 570 |
| Ortega Fat-Free Refried Beans | 9 | 120 | 0 | 570 |
| Rosarita Lowfat Black Bean Refried Beans | 5 | 90 | 0.5 | 460 |
| Rosarita Vegetarian Refried Beans | 6 | 100 | 2 | 500 |
| B&M Original Baked Beans | 6 | 170 | 2 | 380 |
| S&W Chili Beans Zesty Sauce | 6 | 110 | 1 | 580 |
| S&W Santa Fe Beans | 6 | 90 | 0.5 | 680 |

See what I mean about the fiber? Pretty impressive, don't you think?

# Gardenburgers

If you eat a Gardenburger expecting a big beef hamburger, you might be a tad disappointed. But if you're in the mood for something a little different, these great tasting veggie burgers will do the trick. There are all sorts of flavors: Original, Tayburn Smoked Cheddar, Santa Fe, Savory Mushroom, Fire-Roasted Vegetable, and Veggie Medley.

## Gardenburgers

|  | Cal. | Fat[g] (sat. fat) | Fiber[g] | chol.[mg] |
|---|---|---|---|---|
| Fire-Roasted Vegetable | 120 | 2.5(1) | 4 | 15 |
| Original flavor | 130 | 3(1) | 4 | 15 |
| Santa Fe | 130 | 2.5(1) | 4 | 20 |
| Savory Mushroom | 120 | 2.5(1) | 4 | 20 |
| Tayburn Smoked Cheddar | 140 | 3(1.5) | 4 | 10 |
| Veggie Medley | 90 | 0(0) | 3 | 0 |

# Whole-wheat tortillas

Most of you are going to take one look at a package of whole-wheat tortillas and go running as fast as you can toward the traditional white flour tortillas. You have to like whole-wheat and be very motivated to eat fiber to want them. I personally don't mind them if the filling is particularly flavorful, and with just one tortilla you get a whopping nine grams of fiber. For example, La Tortilla Factory's 100% Whole Wheat tortilla contains 60 calories, 9 grams of fiber . . . with no cholesterol and no fat!

# Frozen entrees: some high-fiber surprises

Frozen entrees can come in handy in many situations, whether as a quick lunch during the workweek or as an

# Frozen Entrees with 4 or More Grams of Fiber

| | Cal. | Fat (%*) [g] | Fib. [g] | Sat. fat[g] | Sod. [mg] |
|---|---|---|---|---|---|
| **Frozen Pizza** | | | | | |
| Wolfgang Puck's Mushroom & Spinach Pizza, 1/2 of a 10.5 ounce pizza | 270 | 8 (27%) | 5 | 3 | 380 |
| Wolfgang Puck's Four Cheese Pizza, 1/2 of a 9.25 ounce pizza | 360 | 15 (37%) | 5 | 6 | 530 |
| **Healthy Choice** | | | | | |
| Chicken Enchiladas Suiza | 280 | 6 (19%) | 5 | 3 | 440 |
| Shrimp & Vegetables | 270 | 6 (20%) | 6 | 3 | 580 |
| Herb Baked Fish | 340 | 7 (19%) | 5 | 1.5 | 480 |
| Traditional Breast of Turkey | 290 | 4.5 (14%) | 5 | 2 | 460 |
| Chicken Enchilada Suprema | 300 | 7 (21%) | 4 | 3 | 560 |
| **Lean Cuisine** | | | | | |
| Chicken in Peanut Sauce | 290 | 6 (19%) | 4 | 1.5 | 590 |
| Baked Fish w/ Cheddar Shells | 270 | 6 (20%) | 4 | 2 | 540 |
| Fiesta Chicken (with black beans, rice and vegetables) | 270 | 5 (17%) | 4 | 0.5 | 590 |
| 3-Bean Chili | 250 | 6 (22%) | 9 | 2 | 590 |
| **Marie Calender's** | | | | | |
| Chili & Cornbread | 540 | 21 (35%) | 7 | 9 | 2,110 |
| Sweet & Sour Chicken | 570 | 15 (24%) | 7 | 2.5 | 700 |
| Beef Tips in Mushroom Sc. | 430 | 17 (36%) | 6 | 7 | 1,620 |
| Turkey w/ gravy and dressing | 500 | 19 (34%) | 4 | 9 | 2,040 |
| Spaghetti and Meat Sauce | 670 | 25 (34%) | 9 | 11 | 1,160 |
| Stuffed Pasta Trio | 640 | 18 (25%) | 5 | 9 | 950 |
| **Swanson** | | | | | |
| Mexican Style Combination | 470 | 18 (34%) | 5 | 6 | 1,610 |
| Chicken Parmigiana | 370 | 17 (41%) | 4 | 5 | 1,010 |
| Turkey Dinner | 310 | 8.5 (25%) | 5 | 2 | 890 |

*Percentage of calories from fat

easy dinner if you live alone or with one other person. I usually have a frozen pizza on hand in case of a meal emergency. The problem with frozen entrees is that the ones that are lower in fat are almost always too low in calories, carbohydrates, and vegetables. So in order to make the entrees more nutritious and satisfying, consider adding fruits and vegetables. You might also need to add some cooked rice or noodles, or even grated cheese.

I've listed here the nutrition information for some of the lower-fat frozen entrees that I like and that offer four grams of fiber or more. If you need to watch your sodium intake, keep an eye on the nutrition label, because some frozen entrees have lots of it.

# Losing some of the fat in our favorite foods

I left a couple of brands off the tables in this chapter because they flunked my taste test. If my tasters thought they looked or tasted bad, I left them out. I also don't believe in certain fat-free foods, such as cheese, mayonnaise, margarine, or ice cream. However, there is a brand of fat-free sour cream available that actually beat out the light sour creams in our taste test. Go figure! And as for fat-free cookies and cake, a few rated an "all right," like the fat-free fig bars and angel food cake, but in general, I much prefer a reduced-fat cookie or cake.

# Fat-free but full of calories

When you start reducing fat in favorite foods, the tricky part is making sure you don't eat more of them than you normally would. Fat-free doesn't mean calorie-free and fat-free doesn't mean you can eat the whole box in one sitting. In fact, many of these fat-free products have just as many calories as the full-fat versions. How can that be? In a word: sugar. Sugar, whether it comes from honey, corn syrup, brown sugar, or high-fructose corn syrup, can add moisture and help tenderize bakery products. When added to foods like ice cream, it adds flavor and structure. So I'm not surprised that manufacturers have turned to sugar for assistance while developing reduced-fat and fat-free products. Keep in mind that the majority of the fat-free and lower-fat products on supermarket shelves usually have the same number of calories as the full-fat counterparts (saving us, at most, only 20 calories per serving).

# Fat-free can mean satisfaction-free

Some of us may be using fat-free products as an excuse to overeat. I don't think we are entirely to blame here. If these products aren't as satisfying, we're probably more likely to keep on eating and eating in the hope of reaching some level of satisfaction. Also, some of the advertising has basically encouraged us to eat as much as we want—after all, it's fat-free! So what's a fat-gram and calorie-watching girl to do? *Only select "light" and fat-free products that you truly like* and that satisfy you enough for you to eat modest amounts. Otherwise, don't bother

For example, I really love Cracker Barrel Light Sharp Cheddar. It is real cheese to me. My family enjoys Louis Rich turkey bacon, and we don't miss real bacon. Reduced Fat Bisquick is a staple in my house. We all think Louis Rich Turkey Franks and Ball Park Lite franks taste terrific. These are the types of products you want to keep buying—the ones that you truly enjoy.

Some companies have definitely gone too far.

In my opinion, certain foods simply aren't meant to be fat-free. If you take all the fat out of a food that was mostly fat to begin with, such as mayonnaise, cheese, ice cream, or butter, then what have you really got? Something other than mayonnaise, cheese, ice cream, or butter—that's for sure. It's not fat-free butter, it's just a new kind of yellow goop.

Most of the new fat-free, sugar-free, or "light" products I try end up in the garbage can. However, about 20 percent are keepers. A number of products have successfully hit their optimal level of fat. These are the foods that withstood a modest reduction in fat without a huge loss in taste satisfaction. You'll find them listed in the tables on pages 108 to 116.

# Reduced-fat chips and crunchy snacks

It is hard to go through life without potato chips. Sometimes they just hit the spot, don't they? There are some great-tasting reduced-fat chips out there (not to mention such potato chip alternatives as pretzels and breadsticks). As for the fat-free potato chips made with Olean, you can go for those if you want, but be forewarned—the fat substitute they use can cause intestinal distress in people with normal bowels. I figure if it gives normal people diarrhea, people with IBS symptoms should probably stay clear of it.

# Reduced-fat crackers

Crackers come in handy for a quick snack or as a bed for spreads and cheeses. The problem is that most manufacturers use partially hydrogenated vegetable oils to make them, so much of the fats you find in crackers are saturated or trans fats, which are best avoided. But if you lower the total amount of fat in your cracker, you automatically lower the amount of saturated and trans fats.

The good news is there are now quite a few tasty, reduced-fat crackers to choose from. I've had people taste-test most of the crackers in the chart on page 108, with good reviews.

## Reduced-Fat Chips and Crunchy Snacks

|  | Cal. | Fat(g) | Fib.(g) | Sod.(mg) |
|---|---|---|---|---|
| **Breadsticks (1 stick)** | | | | |
| Stella D'oro Original | 40 | 1 | 0 | 40 |
| Stella D'oro Roasted Garlic | 45 | 1 | 0 | 210 |
| **Chips (per ounce)** | | | | |
| Cape Cod 40% Reduced Fat* | 130 | 6 | 1 | 110 |
| Padrinos Reduced Fat Tortilla | 120 | 4.5 | 2 | 115 |
| Ruffles Reduced Fat | 140 | 7 | 1 | 160 |
| Sun Chips Multigrain French Onion | 140 | 6 | 2 | 160 |
| Tastee Lightly Salted Sweet Potato chips* | 140 | 7 | 2 | 90 |
| **Pretzels (per ounce)** | | | | |
| Snyder's Rods | 120 | 1 | 1 | 290 |
| Snyder's Mini | 110 | 0 | <1 | 250 |

*Made with canola oil

## Reduced-Fat Crackers

|  | Cal. | Fat(g) | Fib.(g) | Sod.(mg) |
|---|---|---|---|---|
| SnackWell's Cracked Pepper (5) | 60 | 1.5 | 0 | 115 |
| SnackWell's Wheat (5) | 70 | 1.5 | <1 | 150 |
| Stoned Wheat Thins Lower Sodium — Red Oval Farms (2) | 60 | 1.5 | <1 | 70 |
| Reduced Fat Club, Keebler (5) | 70 | 2 | 0 | 200 |
| *Reduced Fat Triscuit (8) | 130 | 3 | 4 | 170 |
| Reduced Fat Safeway Select Wheat (6) | 130 | 3 | 1 | 250 |
| Reduced Fat Wheat Thins, (16) | 130 | 4 | 1 | 260 |
| *Reduced Fat Wheatables (13) | 130 | 4 | 2 | 230 |
| Reduced Fat Cheez-It (29) | 140 | 4.5 | <1 | 280 |

*Contain two or more grams of fiber per serving

# Reduced-fat meat products

I love bacon. I'll admit it. But I have to say I am quite satisfied with Louis Rich turkey bacon. I make TLT sandwiches (turkey bacon, lettuce, and tomato) for my family almost weekly, and they love them. The other item we have almost weekly is hot dogs. We tend to go with Louis Rich Turkey Franks and Ball Park Lite franks. Boil them, fry them in a pan with a tiny drizzle of canola oil or cooking spray, or barbecue them. Either way they taste great, even to most hard-core hot dog eaters.

The "meatless" Boca breakfast links also contain two grams of fiber per serving. It is the best-tasting meatless breakfast link I have tasted. (Then again, I had to literally spit out the others.) I thought it tasted all right when smothered with maple syrup and wrapped up in a pancake. My other taste testers rated it "OK" or "pretty bad."

# Reduced-fat dairy products

Fat-free half-and-half? That's right. This is a new product from Land O'Lakes. I tried out this product in my coffee and in a quiche I was making. I usually use whole milk when making a quiche (which is still much lower in fat than cream), but the fat-free half-and-half worked just fine. I haven't yet tried it in candy-making and such, but the carton does say "great for use in baking and cooking." What's in it, you ask? Basically they make it by taking non-fat milk and a tiny bit of whole milk, sweetening it with corn syrup, and pumping in thickener (carrageenan, a fiber from plants that mixes well with water).

When you see fat-free sour cream you probably think, "Why bother?" But there is a brand of fat-free sour cream that actually beat out the reduced-fat (or "light") sour creams in

## Reduced-Fat Meat Products

| | Cal. | Fat[g] (sat fat) | Chol.(mg) | Sod.(mg) |
|---|---|---|---|---|
| **Bacon (per ounce)** | | | | |
| Louis Rich Turkey Bacon, 2 slices | 70 | 5(2) | 30 | 360 |
| Campfire Canadian Style, 2 slices | 25 | 0.75(.25) | 10 | 375 |
| **Hot dogs (per frank)** | | | | |
| Louis Rich | 80 | 6(2) | 40 | 510 |
| Ball Park Lite | 100 | 7(2.5) | 25 | 540 |
| Ball Park Fat Free Smoked White Turkey franks | 40 | 0(0) | 15 | 530 |
| Hebrew National Reduced Fat franks | 120 | 10(4.5) | 25 | 360 |
| **Salami/pepperoni (per ounce)** | | | | |
| Gallo Light Salami | 60 | 4(1.5) | 25 | 520 |
| Hormel Turkey Pepperoni | 80 | 4(1.5) | 40 | 550 |
| **Sausage (per 2 ounces)** | | | | |
| Boca: Breakfast Links, 2 | 80 | 3(0) | 0 | 350 |
| Healthy Choice: Lowfat Smoked Sausage | 80 | 2.5(1) | 25 | 480 |
| Lowfat Polska Kielbasa | 80 | 2.5(1) | 25 | 480 |
| Hillshire Farm: Turkey Polska Kielbasa | 90 | 5(2.5) | 30 | 560 |
| Jimmy Dean: 50% less fat, 2.5 ounces | 170 | 13(4.5) | 50 | 450 |
| Louis Rich: Turkey Smoked Sausage | 90 | 6(1.5) | 35 | 850 |
| Turkey Polska Kielbasa | 90 | 6(1.5) | 35 | 850 |
| The Turkey Store: Mild turkey breakfast Sausage links | 140 | 11(3) | 45 | 360 |

## Reduced-Fat Dairy Products

|  | Cal. | Fat.(g) | Sat. fat(g) |
|---|---|---|---|
| Cream (per 2 tablespoons) | | | |
| Land O'Lakes | | | |
| Fat Free Half-and-Half | 20 | 0 | 0 |
| Carnation Coffee-Mate Fat Free | 20 | 0 | 0 |
| Carnation Coffee-Mate | | | |
| Fat Free French Vanilla | 50 | 0 | 0 |
| International Delight Nondairy | | | |
| Creamer French Vanilla | 60 | 0 | 0 |
| Sour Cream (per 2 tablespoons) | | | |
| Naturally Yours Fat Free Sour Cream | 20 | 0 | 0 |
| Knudsen Light | 40 | 2.5 | 1.5 |

my taste test. It makes a nice ranch dip, and I use it as a fat replacement in brownie, cake, and muffin recipes. Heck, I even top my baked potato with it. It's from the Naturally Yours brand, and you'll know it by the container's black and white cowhide pattern.

# Frozen desserts

I didn't list sugar-free ice creams in the table on page 112 because they usually contain artificial sweeteners, which can encourage intestinal problems for some people. I also bypassed all the fat-free ice creams (unless they were sorbets, which are naturally fat-free) because, frankly, they didn't score well on taste.

# Reduced-fat cheeses

I love cheese. Cheese is my middle name. Because I've never liked milk as a beverage, I probably have gotten most of the calcium in my bones from cheese. I am very pleased to announce there are some wonderful reduced-fat cheeses out there. Some are harder to find than others, like my personal

## Frozen Desserts

| | Cal. | Fat [g] (sat. fat) | Sugar [g] | Chol. [mg] |
|---|---|---|---|---|
| **Starbucks Bars (per bar)** | | | | |
| Frappuccino | 120 | 2(1) | 18 | 10 |
| **Ben & Jerry's Lowfat Frozen Yogurt (per 1/2 cup)** | | | | |
| Cherry Garcia | 170 | 3(2) | 27 | 20 |
| Chocolate Fudge Brownie | 190 | 2.5(1) | 5 | 30 |
| S'mores | 190 | 2(1) | 15 | 26 |
| **Dreyer's Grand Light Ice Cream (per 1/2 cup)** | | | | |
| Peanut Butter Cup | 130 | 5(2.5) | 13 | 20 |
| Vanilla | 100 | 3(2) | 11 | 20 |
| Mint Chocolate Chip | 120 | 4(3) | 13 | 20 |
| Chocolate Fudge Mousse | 110 | 3(2) | 13 | 20 |
| Cookies 'n Cream | 120 | 4(2) | 12 | 20 |
| Cookie Dough | 130 | 5(2.5) | 13 | 20 |
| Coffee Mousse Crunch | 120 | 4(2.5) | 13 | 20 |
| **Sorbet (per 1/2 cup)** | | | | |
| Ben & Jerry's Purple Passion Fruit fat free | 120 | 0(0) | 30 | 0 |
| Haagen-Dazs Raspberry | 120 | 0(0) | 26 | 0 |
| Haagen-Dazs Zesty Lemon | 120 | 0(0) | 28 | 0 |
| Sherbet (per 1/2 cup) | | | | |
| Dreyer's Tropical Rainbow | 130 | 1(0.5) | 24 | 5 |

favorite, Cracker Barrel Light Sharp Cheddar. Maybe as more of us buy reduced-fat cheeses, they will become increasingly available. I've tasted most of the cheeses in the list on page 113 and have been very pleased with them, whether they were filling my lasagna or topping my tortilla.

## Lower-fat cookies

Great-tasting, lower-fat cookies? Yes, it's possible. There really are some good cookies out there that contain less

## Reduced-Fat Cheeses

| | Cal. | Saturated Fat (g) | Fat (g) |
|---|---|---|---|
| **Reduced-fat cheese (per oz. unless otherwise noted)** | | | |
| Precious Low Moisture Part Skim Mozzarella | 80 | 5 | 3 |
| Kraft 2% Milk Reduced Fat Singles (per 2/3 ounce slice) | 45 | 3 | 2 |
| Kraft 2% Milk Reduced Fat Sharp Cheddar | 90 | 6 | 4 |
| Kraft 2% Milk Reduced Fat Monterey Jack | 80 | 6 | 4 |
| Sargento Light 4 Cheese Mexican (1/4 cup) | 70 | 4.5 | 3 |
| Sargento Deli Style Swiss | 80 | 4 | 2.5 |
| **Reduced-fat cream cheese (per ounce)** | | | |
| Philadelphia Fat Free | 30 | 0 | 0 |
| **Ricotta cheese (per 1/4 cup)** | | | |
| Precious Part Skim | 100 | 6 | 4 |

fat and fewer calories. (Fat-free is a different story.) My tasters and I will vouch for most of the cookies listed on page 114, but ultimately you'll have to judge for yourself.

# Pasta sauces

I have listed some store-bought sauces that are great low-fat alternatives on page 115. In order to qualify they had to contain canola or olive oil (the preferred high monounsaturated fat oils). The tomato-based sauces will also contribute those helpful phytochemicals found in cooked tomato products. You can always add extra-lean ground beef, mushrooms, garlic, onion, and spices if you want to dress them up a little.

# Cookies

| | Cookies | Cal. | Fat(g) | Sat. fat(g) | Fiber (g) |
|---|---|---|---|---|---|
| **SnackWell's:** | | | | | |
| Chocolate Chip Bite Size | 13 | 130 | 4 | 1.5 | <1 |
| Double Chocolate Chip Bite Size | 13 | 130 | 4 | 1.5 | 1 |
| Crème Sandwich | 2 | 110 | 3 | 0.5 | 0 |
| Mint Creme | 2 | 110 | 3.5 | 1 | <1 |
| Nabisco Teddy Grahams: | | | | | |
| Chocolate | 24 pc. | 130 | 4.5 | 1 | 1 |
| Chocolatey Chip | 24 pc. | 140 | 4.5 | 1 | <1 |
| Cinnamon | 24 pc. | 130 | 4 | .5 | <1 |
| **Nabisco:** | | | | | |
| Reduced Fat Oreo | 3 | 130 | 3.5 | 1 | 1 |
| Reduced Fat Chips Ahoy | 3 | 140 | 5 | 1.5 | <1 |
| Old Fashioned Ginger Snaps | 4 | 120 | 2.5 | 0.5 | 0 |
| Reduced Fat Chocolate Nilla Wafers | 8 | 110 | 2 | 0 | <1 |
| Barnum's Animals | 10 | 140 | 4 | 0.5 | <1 |
| Fig Newtons | 2 | 110 | 2.5 | 0 | 1 |
| **Mother's:** | | | | | |
| Peach-Apricot Wallops | 1 | 80 | 1.5 | 0.5 | 1 |
| Boysenberry Wallops | 1 | 80 | 1.5 | 0.5 | 1 |
| **Stella D'oro:** | | | | | |
| Anisette Toast Cookies | 3 | 130 | 1 | 0 | <1 |

# Products that might help

## Low-fat yogurt

There are scores of brands and flavors of yogurt in the supermarket. The list on page 116 contains an assortment of the styles and flavors that I found the most interesting. Most of them now contain active yogurt cultures, including *L. acidophilus*, which helps some IBS sufferers. Some brands

# Pasta Sauces

| | Cal. | Fat [g] (sat. fat) | Fib. [g] | Sod. [mg] |
|---|---|---|---|---|
| **Five Brothers:** | | | | |
| Grilled Eggplant and Parmesan | 100 | 3 (0.5) | 3 | 540 |
| Grilled Summer Vegetable | 80 | 3 (0) | 3 | 550 |
| Mushroom and Garlic Grill | 90 | 3 (0) | 3 | 550 |
| Marinara with Burgundy Wine | 90 | 3 (0) | 3 | 480 |
| **Classico:** | | | | |
| Tomato and Basil | 50 | 1 (0) | 2 | 390 |
| Fire-Roasted Tomato and Garlic | 60 | 1 (0) | 2 | 390 |
| Sutter Home: Italian Style (with fresh onions and herbs) | 80 | 2 (0) | 4 | 520 |
| **Barilla:** | | | | |
| Green and Black Olive | 80 | 2.5 (.5) | 3 | 1,010 |
| Roasted Garlic and Onion | 80 | 3.5 (0) | <1 | 460 |
| Mushroom and Garlic | 70 | 2 (.5) | 3 | 610 |
| Tomato and Basil | 70 | 1.5 (.5) | 3 | 640 |
| Marinara | 70 | 2 (.5) | 2 | 430 |

contain artificial sweeteners, cutting the calories and sugar almost in half. These are fine if you aren't sensitive to the artificial sweetener aftertaste.

# Canned fruit

Some people with IBS have noticed that they tend to tolerate well-ripened or canned fruit the best. Obviously, well-ripened fruit isn't available year round, but canned fruit is. Because there are so many choices of fruits canned in juice or light syrup, I thought I'd better list them for you. You can find them on page 117.

## Yogurt (per 6 oz. serving)

| | Calories | Fat (g) | Sugars (g) |
|---|---|---|---|
| **Yoplait Custard Style** | | | |
| Lemon Supreme | 190 | 3.5 | 28 |
| **Yoplait Original 99% Fat Free** | | | |
| Key Lime Pie | | | |
| Orange Creme | | | |
| Tropical Peach | | | |
| Strawberry Mango | | | |
| Banana Creme | 170 | 1.5 | 27 |
| **Yoplait Light** | | | |
| Lemon Cream Pie | | | |
| Very Cherry, | | | |
| Apricot Mango | 100 | 0 | 11 |
| **Dannon Light** | | | |
| White Chocolate Raspberry | | | |
| Blackberry Pie | 90 | 0 | 11 |

# Psyllium products

Psyllium is a naturally grown and harvested grain that is very good at absorbing and holding moisture. In your intestines, the psyllium swells, theoretically forming an easily eliminated stool. Some people swear by psyllium supplements; others say they have little effect.

The Food and Drug Administration recently recognized that diets containing soluble fiber from psyllium husk may reduce the risk of heart disease by lowering cholesterol when included as part of a low-fat diet. You can you find psyllium at a pharmacy or in the medical aisle of your supermarket. In the pharmacy, they'll be with all the other gastrointestinal products. But finding them is the easy part—once you do you'll wonder:

- Which brand do I buy?
- Do I want flavored and artificially sweetened or unflavored?

## Canned Fruit (per 1/2 cup)

| | Calories | Fiber (g) |
|---|---|---|
| **Del Monte:** | | |
| Almond Flavored Apricot Halves in light syrup | 90 | 1 |
| Lite Apricot Halves | 60 | 1 |
| Lite Chunky Mixed Fruit | 60 | 1 |
| Cinnamon Flavored Pear Halves | 80 | 1 |
| Raspberry Flavored Sliced Peaches | 80 | <1 |
| **Dole:** | | |
| Pineapple Chunks in their own juice | 60 | 1 |
| **Geisha:** | | |
| Mandarin Orange in light syrup | 70 | 1 |
| **S&W:** | | |
| Sun Apricots (almond flavored) in light syrup | 90 | 1 |
| Sun Peaches Tropical in light syrup | 80 | 0 |
| Sweet Memory Peaches in light syrup | 80 | <1 |
| Natural Style Fruit Cocktail in lightly sweetened fruit juice | 80 | 2 |
| Natural Style Sliced Bartlett Pears | 80 | 2 |
| Natural Style Sliced Cling Peaches | 80 | 1 |

- If flavored, do I want to try orange or mint?
- Do I want smooth or regular texture?

And you thought it would be simple. So here is some information that might help you in your quest for psyllium.

# Warning

Many of the products warn, "Taking this product without adequate fluid may cause it to swell and block your throat or esophagus and may cause choking. Do not take this product if you have difficulty in swallowing. If you experience chest pain, vomiting, or difficulty in swallowing or breathing after taking this product, seek immediate medical attention." Note that each product is different and you should always read the label before taking any supplements.

# Metamucil

Smooth Texture Metamucil is ground into finer particles than Original Texture Metamucil. They both have the same amount of psyllium and the same efficacy. Metamucil can be taken every day as a dietary fiber supplement when used as directed.

One rounded teaspoonful contains:

- 3.4 grams psyllium fiber.
- < 5 mg sodium.
- 9 calories.

# Perdiem

Make sure you buy the one that says "no chemicals," because the company also makes a Perdiem with laxative stimulants. I tried the mint flavor and it wasn't bad at all. You don't mix it with water like you would some of the other products out there. This fiber therapy generally takes effect after 12 hours (but 48 to 72 hours may be required for optimal relief).

Each rounded teaspoonful contains:

- 4 grams psyllium.
- 36 mg potassium.
- 1.8 mg sodium.
- 4 calories.

# Final thoughts on psyllium supplements

Which product you choose really depends on your preferences. Personally, I would rather just swallow the

Perdiem pellets in one fell swoop (and chase them down with a liquid I actually like) than drink eight ounces of an orange-flavored mixture. But that's just me.

Does it help? I wouldn't say the results have been dramatic, at least for me, though I have had fewer early-morning symptoms. But I think it has been worthwhile, considering that the worst-case scenario is that I increase my soluble fiber intake and perhaps reduce my LDL and total serum cholesterol.

 Chapter 7

# Restaurant Rules

**F**or many people with IBS, including me, eating out can mean intestinal doom. Part of it could be that we tend to eat foods higher in fat when we eat out. Part of it could be that we are served larger portions at restaurants. And part of it could be that when we are treating ourselves to a night on the town, we choose foods we normally don't eat. Any or all of these can spell disaster.

We can make ourselves more comfortable during and after eating out by doing a few things. We can make sure we eat only modest amounts (order conservatively, relax and eat slowly, and remember there are always doggy bags for leftovers). We can choose menu items that aren't too high in fat. And we can stick to dishes that we tend to do well with.

Whether or not you eat modest amounts is entirely up to you, but I can help you choose menu items that are lower in fat—no matter where you eat out.

# Breakfast at the diner

- Ask the restaurant to make your omelet with egg substitute or one egg blended with a few egg whites.
- Skillet potatoes, made with chunks of potato, should (depending on the restaurant) be a little less greasy than hash browns. You can always request that the potatoes be made with a minimum of oil.
- Enjoy a hot cereal of grits or oatmeal. Grits unfortunately won't contribute any fiber, but oatmeal does.
- A plate of buttermilk pancakes with a strip or two of bacon shouldn't get you into too much trouble, as long as you go light on the butter. If you are choosing between a couple of strips of bacon or two links of breakfast sausage, go for the bacon. Even though we think of bacon as fatty, a typical side order of sausage contains even more fat.

# Fast food

For the most part, fast food has a bad reputation in the nutrition department, some of it well deserved. However, some of the chains have made some lower-fat items available, such as grilled chicken sandwiches or Jack in the Box rice bowls. Of course you will still be hard-pressed to find a whole serving of fruit or vegetables, or more than a couple of grams fiber, in the typical fast-food offering.

# Grilled chicken sandwiches

Most of the fast-food grilled chicken sandwiches I've come across are skinless and pretty tasty. But that's where the uniformity ends. Some come on multigrain buns, some with lettuce and tomato, some dressed in barbecue sauce, and some slathered with creamy honey mustard or even mayonnaise.

- The Grilled Chicken Deluxe at McDonald's has 20 grams fat, 440 calories, and 4 grams fiber. But take away the mayo and the fat grams go down to 5 (and the calories go down to 300).
- The Grilled Chicken Sandwich at Wendy's, which comes with reduced calorie honey mustard, contains 8 grams fat, 310 calories, and 2 grams fiber.
- The BK Broiler Chicken Sandwich without mayonnaise totals 9 grams fat, 370 calories, and 2 grams fiber.

# Fish

The good news is that fast-food chains do sell fish. The bad news is that they deep-fry it. But if you eat your fish sandwich without tartar sauce (or at least with most of it scraped off, leaving just enough to wet the bun) you would be surprised to find that when it comes to grams of fat, it can compete with the small hamburger.

- The Burger King fish sandwich (without tartar sauce) contains 14 grams fat, 460 calories, and 3 grams fiber.
- The Filet-O-Fish at McDonald's isn't as big as the Burger King fish sandwich, and without tartar sauce it contains 12 grams fat, 398 calories, and 2 grams fiber.

# Pita sandwiches

Some fast-food chains now feature pita sandwiches that are meals by themselves. Some of these can be fairly low in fat if a reduced-calorie sauce is used, and a source of fiber if vegetables are part of the filling. The pita sandwiches at Wendy's can be made with reduced-fat Caesar vinaigrette (70 calories, 7 grams fat per tablespoon) or reduced-fat garden ranch sauce (50 calories, 4.5 grams fat per tablespoon).

- The Wendy's Garden Veggie Pita contains 17 grams fat, 400 calories, and 5 grams fiber.
- The Wendy's Chicken Caesar Pita contains 18 grams fat, 490 calories, and 4 grams fiber.
- The Wendy's Garden Ranch Chicken Pita contains 18 grams fat, 480 calories, and 5 grams fiber.

# Baked potatoes

Wendy's offers two baked potato options that are worth biting into. They go a long way toward filling you up and contain at least 8 grams fiber.

- The Sour Cream and Chives potato has 6 grams fat, 380 calories, and 8 grams fiber.
- The Broccoli and Cheese Potato contains 14 grams fat, 470 calories, and 9 grams fiber. Still, fewer than 30 percent of the calories come from fat.

# Burgers

When you've just gotta have that burger, make sure it's no larger than a quarter-pounder. And pass up such high-fat toppings and condiments as bacon, cheese, and mayonnaise. Try trimmer ones instead: mustard, catsup, barbecue sauce, lettuce, onion, tomato, and hot peppers (all as tolerated). The smallest hamburgers at fast-food chains (the size that comes in the children's meals) are going to be the better bet for a couple of reasons. They have the least amount of beef per square inch of bun. And they are usually made without mayonnaise or other creamy sauces, which is what the bigger, "deluxe" burgers usually come with. If you're very hungry, these little burgers may not fit the bill. Still, you can always order two!

- The hamburger at Jack in the Box contains 12 grams fat, 280 calories, and 2 grams fiber. The hamburger with cheese contains 16 grams fat, 320 calories, and 2 grams fiber.
- The hamburger at McDonald's has 9 grams fat, 250 calories, and 2 grams fiber; the cheeseburger has 13 grams fat, 320 calories, and 2 grams fiber.
- The Jr. Hamburger at Wendy's has 10 grams fat, 270 calories, and 2 grams fiber and the Jr. Cheeseburger totals 13 grams fat, 320 calories, and 2 grams fiber.
- The hamburger at Burger King contributes 15 grams fat, 320 calories, and 1 gram fiber. Or you can order the Whopper Jr. (without mayonnaise), which has 15 grams fat, 320 calories, and 2 grams fiber.

# Salads

I know, ordering a salad at a fast-food restaurant is almost sacrilege. But salads do add a few grams fiber and will help round out your meal. So if you enjoy salad and if it doesn't provoke IBS symptoms (those with constipation-type IBS may even find that lettuce helps), consider the following:

- The Garden Chicken Salad with low-calorie Italian dressing at Jack in the Box adds up to 200 calories, 9 grams fat, and 3 grams fiber.

- The Grilled Chicken Salad with half a package of Caesar dressing at McDonald's totals 200 calories, 8.5 grams fat, and 3 grams fiber.
- A Caesar Side Salad at Wendy's has 110 calories, 5 grams fat, and 1 gram of fiber. A Deluxe Garden Salad has 110 calories, 6 grams fat, and 3 grams fiber. A Grilled Chicken Salad has 200 calories, 8 grams fat, and 3 grams fiber. Two tablespoons of reduced-fat Italian dressing add 40 calories and 3 grams fat.

# Taco Bell and Mexican restaurants

Although the nutritional information that follows is specific to the Taco Bell chain, the food tips may help you in other Mexican fast-food chains or restaurants.

## Soft tacos

A soft taco is made with a soft, flour tortilla, rather than a crispy (fried) corn tortilla. No matter where you are, a soft taco is usually going to be lower in fat than a crispy taco. At Taco Bell, these are the lower-fat soft tacos:

- Grilled Steak Soft Taco, which has 200 calories, 7 grams total fat, 2.5 grams saturated fat, and 2 grams fiber.
- Grilled Chicken Soft Taco, which has 200 calories, 7 grams total fat, 2.5 grams saturated fat, and 2 grams fiber.

## Burritos

Burritos are typically made with large flour tortillas and are not fried (although you can get them fried in some restaurants). Depending on which fillings you choose, they can have double the fat and one quarter the fiber of the lowest-fat burrito, the bean burrito.

- Bean Burrito, which has 370 calories, 12 grams fat, 3.5 grams saturated fat, and 12 grams fiber.
- Grilled Chicken Burrito, which has 390 calories, 13 grams fat, 4 grams saturated fat, and 3 grams fiber.

## Sandwiches

Sandwiches are usually well tolerated (depending on their contents). Request whole-wheat bread, rolls, or bagels to pump up the fiber in your sandwich when you can. If you are bothered by gas and bloating, skip sandwiches stuffed with vegetables.

- Hold the mayo. Order your sandwich with catsup or mustard. Sometimes Italian delis will lightly wet the bread with an olive oil mixture, which at least adds the more desirable monoun- saturated fat. If you must have mayonnaise, ask that they spread it very lightly.
- Choose leaner meats. Roast chicken, roast turkey, and roast beef are all great choices; a lean ham will also do well.
- When it comes to chicken, shrimp, or tuna salad, you are better off enjoying a light version made at home. Restaurants and delis usually make these salads with generous amounts of mayonnaise.

## Pizza

I have to admit that I'm partial to pizza. My family probably orders or makes pizza once a week. Nearly everybody has a favorite pizza chain, some of which make greasier pizza than others. Basically, the more authentically Italian your pizza is (made with a breadier crust and light on the cheese), the lower in fat the crust will be. That's half the battle. The other half is how you top that crust. Don't use gobs of cheese, and avoid fatty, spicy meats, which can get you into trouble very quickly. If at all possible, order your pizza with vegetable toppings you like and tolerate well. If you are a meat lover, your best bet is Canadian bacon or lean ham.

Another important trick to pizza is quitting while you're ahead. It's easy to eat slice after slice of pizza until you are stuffed. Stick to two large slices in one sitting. If you are still hungry, have some fruit, a bowl of soup, or a green salad as tolerated.

# The rotisserie

- Enjoy sliced turkey breast or lean ham with new potatoes, steamed vegetables, and hot cinnamon apples and your bill will ring up to around 595 calories, with 9 grams fat and 2 grams saturated fat.
- If you opt for the roasted chicken, skip the skin (that's where most of the fat is) or just eat a few bites of the crispy bits you can't resist and toss the rest.
- Pass up such creamy side dishes as creamed spinach and ask for the baked new potatoes or sweet potatoes, zucchini marinara, rice pilaf, red beans and rice, steamed vegetables, or fresh fruit.
- The meatloaf sandwich (without cheese) should keep your fat in check, especially if you have it with a low-fat soup and/or fruits and vegetables.

- Chicken noodle soup (and most other clear soups) with corn bread can make a nice light lunch or dinner.

## The steakhouse

The trouble with eating at steakhouses is that not only are many foods deep-fried and/or high in fat, but also that most of the time you saddle up to cowboy-sized servings. You can plan ahead and make yourself more comfortable after the meal by finding items you enjoy that are better, leaner choices, and making sure you eat only until you are comfortably full. Don't overdo it.

- The lean cuts of beef available at steakhouses are usually sirloin or filet mignon (the fatter cuts are rib eye, prime rib, porterhouse, and T-bone).
- Order the "petite" or "junior" portions of meat when available.
- Trim all visible fat from whichever cut of meat you choose.
- Have your meat dish with lots of vegetables that you tolerate well (beans if you are able). The vegetables will help fill you up so you won't be tempted to overdo the meat, and the vegetables and beans help boost fiber totals, too.
- Eat side dishes that you tolerate well and that are lower in fat to help balance out the beef. These might include a clear broth or tomato-based soup, baked potato (modest on butter and sour cream) or mashed potatoes, broccoli, beans, rice pilaf, dinner roll, corn bread, and cinnamon apples.

# Contemporary cuisine tips

- Grilled or roasted chicken and fish are two of the healthiest things you can order at many restaurants.
- Ask that the skin be removed from your chicken before it is prepared.
- Order leaner cuts of beef. Top sirloin and filet mignon are good choices.
- High-fat, buttery, or creamy sauces should be garnishes, not large portions of the meal. Ask for half as much of these sauces when ordering pasta or meat dishes.
- If you really want a dish that is sautéed or simmered in cream or butter, ask that it be simmered in wine or broth instead.
- Ask to substitute marinara, marsala, or wine sauces for cream and butter sauces that come with chicken, fish, or pasta.

# Casual cuisine tips

- Ask for salad dressing on the side. This way you decide how much you add to your salad.
- Ask for grilled chicken instead of fried.
- Some of our favorite comfort foods, like pot roast or turkey dinners, are actually some of the lower-fat and better-tolerated entrees at restaurants.
- Grilled chicken breast is always a good choice at a restaurant.
- Grilled fish is a great dinner choice. Not only does fish contain beneficial omega-3 fatty acids, it is also the type of dinner we tend to not make for ourselves at home.

## Chinese restaurants

In general, you may have to avoid items marked hot and spicy. Garlic, curry, hot peppers, and ginger can give some people problems. You can easily avoid the hot peppers and curry by ordering items that don't contain them, but it is more difficult to avoid garlic and ginger, both of which seem to be in almost everything. If you can tolerate a little of either, then perhaps all you need to do is avoid the dishes that have ginger or garlic in their titles (such as garlic shrimp or ginger beef).

The other group of menu items to steer clear of are deep-fried items. Like most rich foods, they can wreak havoc on your intestines. Stir-fried dishes tend to be well tolerated by most with IBS, but I would guess that the higher the amount of oil used in the stir-fry, the greater the potential discomfort and after effects.

## Japanese restaurants

IBS sufferers usually do well with rice, fish, and grilled or broiled meats, so all those wonderful grilled dishes in Japanese restaurants are probably a good bet. Japanese noodle soups and the standard miso soup should also be fine.

Tempura, the one dish that causes me trouble in Japanese restaurants, is also my favorite (funny how that works). But I've learned that if I only eat four pieces or so (about half an order) I seem to be fine. Of course, I'm eating the tempura with soup and lots of rice. If I eat the entire entrée (which is easy to do because it tastes so wonderful), I'm done for.

# Italian restaurants

If you are not bothered by tomatoes, you will have many choices at Italian restaurants. Any entrée made with lean meat or vegetables and marinara sauce might work well. If you like pasta with cream sauce, keep your portions very small and enjoy less rich (and higher-fiber if possible) side dishes with it, such as bread, soup, and vegetables.

# Mediterranean restaurants

People in the Mediterranean like their fish and shellfish. Fish is usually well tolerated by people with IBS, and it's even better for you if you eat it with some rice and in-season vegetables. Olive oil and olives are also a big part of Mediterranean cuisine. This might only be a problem if you eat a large amount of olive oil at one time.

# Chez moi

I love going to restaurants. What's not to like? But when you have IBS, you can pay dearly for the fun of eating out. If you follow the tips in this chapter, you may well spare yourself future discomfort.

If you want to lighten up some of the most popular recipes from famous restaurants in your own kitchen, you might be interested in one of my cookbooks, *Chez Moi: Lightening Up Famous Restaurant Recipes*. It's full of sought-after restaurant recipes that I've turned into reduced-fat treasures.

# Glossary

**antacid**  An agent that counteracts acidity in the stomach, such as calcium carbonate or sodium bicarbonate.

**carbohydrate**  Organic molecules that are broken down during the process of metabolism providing the main energy source for the body.

**carcinogen**  An agent that can cause cancer.

**cholesterol**  A waxy substance produced by the liver and found in certain foods. It is needed to make vitamin D and some hormones, helps you digest fat, and build cell walls. But too much of the wrong kind of cholesterol (LDL) can lead to blockages in the arteries.

**constipation**  The inability to have or infrequency of bowel movements.

**dehydration**  An abnormal shortage of body fluids.

**dietitian**  A professional nutrition expert who can develop a modified diet that can lead to a healthier lifestyle.

**distention**  The state  of being enlarged or swollen from internal pressure.

**enzymes**  Proteins that catalyze chemical reactions that convert one type of molecule to another.

**fibromyalgia** Condition characterized by widespread pain in the muscles, ligaments, and tendons.

**fructose** A simple sugar that can be found in small amounts in fruits and vegetables but can be found in higher amounts in processed foods.

**gastroenterologist** A physician who specializes in the diagnosis and treatment of the disorders of the gastro-intestinal tract, including the esophagus, stomach, small intestine, large intestine, pancreas, liver, gallbladder, and biliary system.

**glycerol** A syrupy alcohol, also called glycerin.

**hydrogenated oil** An oil that is made by forcing hydrogen into oil at high pressure, making the oil a solid. These kinds of oils can be found in oleo and margarines.

**hypermotility** Excessive movement in the gastro–intestinal tract.

**lactose** A sugar found in milk.

**Olestra** A non-fat cooking oil that is made by chemically combining sugar and the fatty acids obtained from vegetable oils.

**psyllium** Parts of the seeds of a specific plant that increases bulk in the digestive track by adding a high amount of fiber.

**sorbitol** A sugar alcohol derived from glucose.

**spasm** A sudden, sometimes painful, involuntary contraction of a muscle, group of muscles, or a hollow organ.

# For More Information

American Dietetic Association
120 South Riverside Plaza, Suite 2000
Chicago, IL 60606-6995
Phone: (800) 877-1600
Web site: http://www.eatright.org
The largest organization of food and nutrition professionals
in the United States.

American Heart Association                              ,
National Center
7272 Greenville Avenue
Dallas, TX 75231
Phone: (800) 242-8721
Web site: http://www.americanheart.org
An association dedicated to building healthier lives, free of
cardiovascular diseases and stroke.

Irritable Bowel Syndrome Association
1440 Whalley Avenue, #145

New Haven, CT 06515

Web site: http://www.ibsassociation.org

E-mail: ibsa@ibsassociation.org

An organization dedicated to helping everyone who suffers from IBS through patient support groups, treatment, accurate information, and education.

# Web sites

Due to the changing nature of Internet links, Rosen Publishing has developed an online list of Web sites related to the subject of this book. This site is updated regularly. Please use this link to access the list:

http://www.rosenlinks.com/tmwe/ibsy

# For Further Reading

Bonci, Leslie. *American Dietetic Association Guide to Better Digestion*. Hoboken, NJ: Wiley, 2003.

Burstall, Dawn, T. Michael Vallis, and Geoffrey K. Turnbull. *I.B.S. Relief: A Doctor, a Dietitian, and a Psychologist Provide a Team Approach to Managing Irritable Bowel Syndrome*. Hoboken, NJ: Wiley 1998.

Carper, Steve. *Milk Is Not for Every Body: Living with Lactose Intolerance*. New York, NY: Plume, 1996.

Dahlman, David. *Why Doesn't My Doctor Know This? Conquering Irritable Bowel Syndrome, Inflammatory Bowel Disease, Crohn's Disease, and Colitis*. Garden City, NY: Morgan James Publishing, 2008.

Darnley, Simon, and Barbara Millar. *Understanding Irritable Bowel Syndrome*. Hoboken, NJ: Wiley, 2003.

Lacy, Brian E. *Making Sense of IBS: A Physician Answers Your Questions About Irritable Bowel Syndrome*. Baltimore, MD: Johns Hopkins, 2006.

Lipski, Elizabeth. *Digestive Wellness*. New York, NY: McGraw-Hill, 2004.

Miskovitz, Paul, M.D. *The Doctor's Guide to Gastrointestinal Health: Preventing and Treating Acid Reflux, Ulcers,*

*Irritable Bowel Syndrome, Diverticulitis, Celiac Disease . . . and More*. Hoboken, NJ: Wiley, 2005.

Nicol, Rosemary. *Irritable Bowel Syndrome: A Natural Approach*. Berkeley, CA: Ulysses Press, 2007.

O'Hare, Laura. *The Irritable Bowel Sourcebook*. New York, NY: McGraw-Hill, 2001.

Van Vorous, Heather. *The First Year: IBS—An Essential Guide for the Newly Diagnosed*. New York, NY: Marlowe, 2005.

# Index

## A

Abdominal bloating/
    swelling, 27
Abdominal pain, 24–25
Alcohol, 65

## B

Baked potatoes, 123
Beans, 102
Bladder problems, 29
Bowel movements, 9–10,
    21, 25
Bran, 40
BRAT diet, 37
Breads, 99, 100

Breakfast, 121
Burgers, 123–124

## C

Caffeine,
    amounts in beverages, 58
    limiting, 57–58
Cancer, 19
    preventing, 45
Cereals, 99, 101
Cheeses, 111, 113
*Chez moi*, 131
Chest pain, 29
Chinese restaurants, 130
Chocolate, 35
Colitis, 19, 27

Constipation, 51–53
Cookies, 112–113, 114
Crackers, 107–108

# D

Dairy products, 109–111
Defecation,
  irregular patterns of, 25
Diarrhea, 51–53
  preventing, 32–33
Diet,
  BRAT, 37
  changes in, 31
Digestion, 9–10, 20–21, 28
Digestive tract, 20–21
Distention, 13, 39

# E

Eating, 13
  habits, 38–39, 67–68, 120
Exercise, 68–69

# F

Fast food, 38, 121–124
Fat,
  ideal threshold of, 59–60,
    62–63
  reducing in foods, 37–38,
    58–64, 105–114
  replacements for, 60–61,
    62–64

Fatigue, 29
FFS journal, 31, 48–50
Fiber, 31, 39, 49, 51–56
  bran, 40
  content in food, 99–105
  fitting into diet, 55–56
  insoluble, 53–54
  psyllium, 52–53
  role in intestines, 51
  soluble, 39, 40, 53
  tips, 53
  types of, 55
Fibromyalgia, 29
Flavonoids, 53
Fluids, 37
Food steps to freedom, 47–69
Foods,
  allergies, 20
  fat-free, 105–107
  gas producing, 28, 66–67
  helpful for IBS, 37,
    114–118
  high-fiber, 49, 51, 54
  suspect, 32
  tolerated by bowels,
    fruits, 37
  vegetables, 36
  trigger, 31, 32, 33–34
Frozen desserts, 111, 112
Frozen entrees, 103–105
Fructose, 34
Fruits and vegetables,
    36–37, 46, 55, 56
  canned, 117

## G

Gardenburgers, 103
Gas attacks, 28
Gastrointestinal (GI) tract, 68

## H

Heartburn, 28, 35, 37
Herbs, 40
Hormones, 15
Hypnosis, 19

## I

Intestinal attacks, 23
Intestinal space, 26–27
Introduction, 7–11
Irritable bowel syndrome,
  and eating style, 38–39
  and genetics, 15
  and psychotherapy, 18
  and traveling, 22
  causes, 14, 16–17
  constipation
    predominant, 25–26
  definitions of, 7, 12
  diarrhea-predominant,
    26–27
  foods, 13, 30–46
  history of, 8
  lack of sleep and, 21
  lactose intolerance and,
    41–45

meal size and, 67–68
medication effecting,
  16–17, 22
signs of, 14
statistics of, 8
stress and anxiety, 10, 18,
  30, 32
symptoms of, 12–13, 19,
  21, 24–30
treatments of, 8
Italian restaurants, 131

## J

Japanese restaurants, 130

## L

Lactose and lactase, 41,
  43, 44
  hidden, 44–45
  lactase tablets, 43
Lactose intolerance, 41–45
  steps in preventing, 42–43
  symptoms, 41–42
Laxatives, 17
Lignans, 53

## M

Meat products, 109, 110
Medicines, 13, 26

making IBS worse, 17
to use when traveling, 22
Mediterranean
  restaurants, 131
Metamucil, 118
Mexican food, 125–126
Migraine headaches, 29
Minerals, 53

## N

Nausea, 29
Navigating the
  supermarket, 97–119

## O

Olestra, 35

## P

Pasta sauces, 113, 115
Perdiem, 118
Pizza, 126–127
Psychotherapy, 18
Psyllium, 52–53
  allergies to, 52
  products, 116–118

## R

Recipes, 70–96
Rectum,
  incomplete emptying
    of, 27
Restaurant rules, 120–131
  contemporary cuisine
    tips, 129
  casual cuisine tips, 129
Rotisserie restaurants,
  127–128

## S

Salads, 124–125
Sandwiches, 126
  fish sandwiches, 122
  grilled chicken
    sandwiches, 121–122
  pita sandwiches, 123
Saponins, 53
Sleep disturbances, 29
Snacks, 107, 108
Soft drinks, 34
Sorbitol, 34
Spices,
  avoiding certain, 65–66
Steakhouses, 128

Stress, 10, 18, 32, 48–49
  reduction, 18
  sources of, 10
Symptoms, 24–30, 47
  during menstruation, 28
  food provoking, 32, 33
  non–bowel related, 29, 48
  other than IBS, 19–20, 21
  reducing, 10–11
  related to diet, 30–31, 32,
    33–36, 38–39

## T

Tocotrienols, 53
Trigger foods, 31, 32

## U

Urinary problems, 29

## V

Vitamin C, 36
Vitamin E, 53

## W

Waffles, 101
Water, 55, 56–57
Whole-wheat tortillas, 103

## Y

Yogurt, 114, 116

# About the Author

Elaine Magee, M.P.H., R.D., is the author of the celebrated syndicated column "The Recipe Doctor." Elaine is a regular contributor to *Parenting* and *Woman's Day* and is the author of eighteen books on nutrition and cooking, including *The Recipe Doctor* as well as the previous books in the *Tell Me What to Eat* series. She has her own Web site (recipedoctor.com) and contributes to several Web sites, including dietriot.com.